Barker's Grub

THREE RIVERS PRESS • NEW YORK

Barker's Grub

Easy, Wholesome
Home Cooking

Rudy Edalati

Foreword by
Dr. Jean Hofve

Published by Three Rivers Press, New York, New York.
Member of the Crown Publishing Group.

Random House, Inc. New York, Toronto, London, Sydney, Auckland
www.randomhouse.com

Three Rivers Press is a registered trademark and
the Three Rivers Press colophon is a trademark of Random House, Inc.

Design by Lynne Amft

Printed in the United States of America

Library of Congress Cataloging-in-Publication Data is available on request.

ISBN: 0-609-80442-1

10 9 8 7 6 5

For my grandmother

Rohanniẽ,
a brilliant lady

———

And in memory of

charly

Contents

Chapter 6

Barker's Grub Recipes / *115*

Acknowledgments

I would first like to thank Caroline Casey, without whom this book would never have been possible. It was her belief in my recipes and approach to nutrition, as a loyal friend and client, which originally brought my work at Barker's Grub to the attention of Three Rivers Press.

I am enormously grateful to my dear friend and mentor, Dr. Michael W. Fox, one of the world's deepest souls. He has always fed my curiosity about animal nutrition with practical information and most generously shares his personal and professional resources. Thanks, Mikey!

My deep gratitude extends to Stephanie Gunning, whose enormous talent as a writer and amazing editorial vision guided me through the process of creating this work. She held my hand through the rough spots and anxious moments, and her wonderful insights and patience gave me courage to set my ideas down in print.

My family has always been a tremendous support, especially my mother, Parvin, and my brother, Cameron. Without them I would not have started or maintained my cooking business, much less have written this book.

Many thanks to Sarah Silbert, my editor, and the wonderful staff at Three Rivers Press, who saw this project through to completion; and also to Steven Magnuson and Jessica Schulte, who initiated it. And Lynda Bamzi for the photos.

Dr. Monique Maniet of Veterinary Holistic Care of Bethesda, Maryland, took a chance on me when I opened Barker's Grub. Her belief in the power of nutrition is a constant inspiration.

I am also indebted to Dr. Grace Calabrese and Dr. Leslie Taylor, two exceptional veterinarians, for giving valuable time and consideration to this project; their expertise helped me navigate its creation. I also respect their work with shelter animals.

My appreciation extends to readers Sara J. Whitcomb, Joel Finkelstein, David Powers, Melanie Patt-Corner, and Jean Hofve, DVM, of the Animal Protection Institute, for commenting on various drafts of the manuscript and for the wonderful foreword.

Thanks to my wonderful and loyal clients at Barker's Grub without whom there would be no recipes or stories to share.

And finally, I would like to thank the animals in my life: my dogs Hannah, Oscar, George, and their foster packmate, Ginger, for their constant unconditional love and emotional support; my horse, Haley, one of the most important teachers of my life; and my cats, Edgar, Pufang, Cheeba, and Trang-Doo, for their warmth and affection.

Foreword

Over the last ten years or so, people's interest in nutrition has increased exponentially, not just for ourselves, but also for our companion animals. There are dozens of dog diet gurus, each claiming to be the last, best word on the subject. Many of these diets are complex and cumbersome, some less than palatable, some downright dangerous. Into the fray steps Rudy Edalati, with her simple, commonsense recipes. She has reclaimed her elders' nutritional knowledge: that good, wholesome, nutritious food must come first if we want to see our dogs express their most healthy and vital selves.

From the cheapest generic kibble to the expensive medical diets, commercial pet foods are highly processed and treated with chemicals and additives to make them "complete" as well as palatable. Nutrients that are destroyed by processing are replaced with synthetic equivalents. Most dry foods contain powerful synthetic antioxidants to give them a long shelf life. For the most part, they contain animal organs and parts deemed "not fit for human consumption." Do pet food manufacturers really think that ingredients that are too unhealthy for people to eat are good for dogs? Or that food from bags that have been sitting in a warehouse for a year or more is wholesome fare?

In fact, they are not. Many people have discovered, to their dismay, that processed pet foods have damaged their animals. Allergies, ear infections, diabetes, pancreatitis, inflammatory bowel disease, dull coats, dandruff, lethargy, dental disease—

all have dietary links. While diet is not the sole cause of disease, it is clear that the body—human or canine—cannot maintain itself, let alone heal itself, without "good groceries."

When we bring a dog into our lives and homes, we assume full responsibility for his physical and emotional needs. Adoption includes a commitment to tend to our dog's needs for shelter, water, exercise, affection, training, play, and food. To us, dogs aren't second-class citizens; they are members of our family. Therefore, we should put as much thought and care into what goes into his bowl as into ours. Rudy has made this part of canine care, at least, easy and fun. Most of the recipes can be prepared right along with food we are fixing for ourselves, with very little extra effort. Feeding dogs really is a lot like feeding ourselves and our children. We would never consider a diet consisting entirely of processed foods from cans, boxes, and bags to be healthy for us—and it's really no different for our dogs. For all of us, a return to the basics, to a more wholesome, "natural" diet, makes the most sense.

Critics may disparage the lack of "scientific" verification of the recipes in this book. Let the critics take a good look at the standards by which commercial pet food is made. How many dogs and cats have sickened or even died from commercial foods, while nutritionists struggled to understand how much of what nutrients really ought to be included? Today, we know how much of each vitamin and mineral will prevent overt deficiency diseases, and how much might be toxic. But no one really knows what the optimal diet for our companion animals looks like. I suspect it doesn't look very much like kibble.

The proof of the pudding is definitely in the eating. If you feed your dog the recipes in this book, as part or all of her diet, you will see a change for the better. Rudy has seen it in her dogs, and in dozens of clients' dogs. If you're anything like me, when you start cooking for your animals, you'll end up eating better yourself. It's a win-win situation. Enjoy!

Dr. Jean C. Hofve
veterinarian, animal advocate, and author
Sacramento, California
October 2000

Barker's Grub

Introduction

WHY I BEGAN TO COOK FOR DOGS

There is so much confusion today about what to feed dogs. Pet food can be as tricky a subject as human food—there seem to be so many dos and don'ts. Most of us would love to believe that science has evolved to the point where every nutritional question has been answered, that experts have done the work for us, and that we can purchase health and well-being in a can or bag. I am sorry to report, it simply is not so. Most veterinarians, with the exception of holistic veterinarians, study only a few hours on the topic of nutrition in veterinary school. There are very few veterinary nutritionists out there—forty-four in the entire United States at the time of this book's publication. Those who have explored the topic of canine nutrition advocate home cooking, but you're pretty much on your own to figure out the appropriate ingredients and quantities. So, where can we turn for practical advice? We dog lovers must rely largely on common sense.

My goal in this book is to simplify the subject of dog nutrition and make feeding your four-legged companions an occasion of daily joy and satisfaction. I have spent the past five years building a dog food catering business called Barker's Grub, in the greater Washington, DC, and suburban Maryland area, with that one aim in mind. Like you, I love, respect, and live with animals—currently four dogs and five cats. And I believe there should be no mystery in good, wholesome meals for dogs. Since establishing my business, I have worked closely with several local holistic veterinarians and their canine patients, both as a preventive and as a restorative health measure. Still the greatest reward I have found in my work is the enormous pleasure dogs take in eating the recipes I am sharing with you here.

My eyes were opened to the power of home cooking for my dogs through an intense personal experience. When I first decided to adopt a dog, I became very excited. I had grown up around animals; we had dogs and cats at home and I worked for years with horses in a stable. The only difference was that this puppy would be my complete responsibility. Because I wanted to do everything right, I did homework on dog-proofing the house and finding a knowledgeable veterinarian. In addition, I educated myself on other basics of responsible pet ownership, such as spay/neuter programs, licenses, and vaccines. Then I went to the pound and rescued a mixed-breed puppy that caught my eye and named her Hannah. It was love at first sight.

After the puppy got her shots, the veterinarian sent me home with a supply of pricey brand-name dog food. That should have been the end of this story: "They lived happily ever after!" But there were many problems ahead of us.

Not long after I adopted my dog Hannah, I noticed that her coat was dull and getting worse, and she was emitting a weird body odor. Initially, I attributed Hannah's poor coat and odor to bad grooming, a lack of proper nutrition in the shelter, and just not getting the attention she had needed while she was in the pound. I tried bathing her with expensive shampoos I purchased from the vet, but no amount of washing seemed to remedy the problem. More frustrating still was that even after performing a skin scrape test, the vet couldn't pinpoint the source and reason behind Hannah's foul smell.

Finally, one evening, I noticed Hannah wasn't feeling too good—she didn't seem her normal playful self. She started losing her equilibrium an hour or so later, and her pupils became dilated. Minutes after, she began vomiting violently. I immediately rushed her to the local emergency animal hospital, where she was put under observation for what seemed like hours. After some tests, the attending veterinarian told me Hannah had some sort of "toxicity," but couldn't give me a straight answer as to what had caused "toxins" to accumulate in her body. Needless to say, I was dumbfounded.

The next day I took Hannah home and at the vet's suggestion put her on a bland diet of chicken and white rice. He told me that if all went well, after a week she could go back on her regular food. I called my mom for her advice, because I could remember her feeding special dishes to our pets when I was a kid, and she gave me a couple of simple recipe ideas. Ten days later, Hannah seemed well, and life in our household went back to the way things were before; I took my dog off homemade food and put her back on her specially formulated commercial diet.

A couple of days later the same type of episode recurred. Back to the vet we went. This time, because of my experiment with home cooking—and because I had watched Hannah closely in the intervening period to make sure she wasn't getting into cleaning products or ingesting other unnatural substances—it was more obvious that the toxins came from something she was eating in her regular diet. After carefully watching Hannah over the next few days, I noticed nothing remarkable about her food intake. It was just the highly recommended dog food I bought at the veterinary clinic. Eventually, I put two and two together and realized that it had to be the commercial food I was giving her that was causing the problem.

Bewildered and in shock, I couldn't believe that this so-called scientifically formulated brand of pet food was the source of my agony, not to mention the tremendous harm it had brought on my beloved Hannah. I had unwittingly put my trust in processed pet food, and I felt like a complete idiot. The question kept passing through my mind, "How could I have been so out of tune with my dog's needs and my own basic instincts?" That day I lost my blind faith in science and in commercial pet food. I realized that vets aren't gods. They are human beings; and just like everyone else, they aren't perfect and all knowing.

More significantly, as a result of Hannah's crisis, I began to question what pet food really is. Who makes it? What are the ingredients? Does it come from the moon? Does it have magical power? The answers I found made a resounding NO. Pet food is generally processed scraps and meat and other human-food-industry by-products doused with loads of preservatives and cooked at extremely high temperatures. Then why was that vet so eager to push this stuff on me? The answer was that he didn't know any better. (Plus, it probably didn't hurt his pocketbook to promote such products.)

As a result of my outrage and concern, I found I had a burning desire to learn as much as I could about my dog's health and well-being as it related to food. Thus I began an intense search for the truth about various ingredients. I took the knowledge I had picked up by reading on the subject and started cooking for Hannah. I originally worried that it would be an arduous chore, but it didn't take as much time as I thought it would to whip up a batch each week. Much to my surprise I also found I enjoyed cooking for her immensely. In fact, I loved it! And mostly I loved it because of the health and joy it brought my Hannah.

To make a long story short, I've been cooking for animals ever since. Yes, me, a person who once dreaded cooking for myself, let alone anyone else. In fact, Hannah and I started eating right together, and I discovered true joy in making my sweet dog happy. Within a couple of years I adopted two more dogs and three cats. Nowadays, the animal population in my house goes up and down according to what rescued dog or cat needs fostering at any given moment. Knowing that my pets are receiving the best nutrition from a complete and balanced meal gives me pleasure, and I am satisfied because I know I am doing the right thing for them.

When my friends and family learned how well my dogs were thriving on my homemade food, they came around for lessons and supplies. Soon I was giving away huge quantities every week. Finally, I asked myself, "Why not cook for dogs as a business?" I opened Barker's Grub (named by my brilliant brother) with a handful of customers. To drum up more business, I contacted a couple of local holistic veterinarians and presented my ideas in long conversations. Dr. Monique Maniet immediately took a chance on me. She began sending me clients whose dogs had specific ailments. Word of mouth spread, and other vets soon contacted me. In these five years, I have met many wonderful and caring veterinarians who emanate such an amazingly positive energy and interest in nutrition that I feel a great sense of hope for the direction animal medicine is moving.

My grandmother Rohanniẽ had age-old knowledge about food and nutrition that she passed on to my mother, starting when my mother was pregnant with me. She taught my mother that proper nutrition would form the fetus physically and mentally, preparing it for life, and she made a point of eating well, drinking good water, and surrounding herself with beautiful flowers and artwork. She taught us that your body reacts chemically through the emotions to these things in the environment. I have tried my best to incorporate all those elements into the philosophy and structure of this book.

Holistic Pet Care:
Complementary Medicine for Dogs

Holistic veterinary medicine is an idea whose time has definitely come. In recent years, we in America have rediscovered—and begun to accept into the mainstream—the principles of holistic health care and sound nutrition for human beings. Why not for animals? In fact, you can find practitioners of this growing veterinary specialization in every region of the country.

Over the years, I have seen and learned about numerous cases of dogs whose conditions have been successfully treated by nontraditional therapies. Dogs respond well to acupuncture, chiropractic care, and homeopathy. Combined with sound nutritional principles, holistic veterinary care is amazingly effective, but you have to be patient and willing to work with the veterinarian, and not give up if you do not see results overnight. Holistic medicine is not attempting to cure isolated symptoms; it is centered on bringing the whole body into a balanced state of optimal well-being. This is a lifelong enterprise. And the holistic veterinarians with whom I have spoken uniformly believe that proper nutrition is essential to promote good health.

Veterinarian Michael W. Fox, syndicated columnist, and author of *Understanding Your Dog,* is a strong advocate of homemade diets and whole foods. When he is at the dog park with his three dogs, people have been known to stop him and remark, "Your dogs shine." If they want to know how he keeps his dogs so vibrant, Fox, who cooks for his dogs, tells them, "Use natural food ingredients and flaxseed oil. I was told many years ago as a child in England that these were the best things to make a dog strong and for it to have a good coat."

When a holistic veterinarian is working to make a diagnosis of a dog's condition, in addition to the physical and behavioral

Barker's Grub

symptoms that indicate an underlying problem, he or she takes into account the dog's family history, genetic background and breed susceptibility, vaccination history, and dietary regimen. Because the dog's genetic makeup obviously cannot be changed, the holistic vet assesses the vaccination protocols and modifies its diet, putting a dog on special homemade foods and supplements formulated to deal with its specific diagnosed condition, such as kidney disease, allergies, arthritis, or congestive heart failure. Additionally, the vet may prescribe homeopathic remedies, herbs, and chiropractic or acupuncture sessions to alleviate symptoms—even drugs and surgery when indicated.

There is nothing like a good veterinarian, one who cares about your dog almost as much as you do. Most veterinarians truly love and respect animals. This health-care provider is someone with whom you need to be able to exchange ideas, who is willing to discuss alternative therapies and new forms of medicine, and who places consideration of the dog above all other things, including generating his or her own income.

How can you know which veterinarian is the right one for your dog? There are a number of legitimate considerations including degrees, certification and experience, and membership in peer organizations, as well as general broad-mindedness and likability. Be prepared to ask your veterinarian his or her ideas about your dog's nutritional requirements and food sources. Does the vet advocate fresh food versus processed food? Does he or she have views about supplementation? You need to be satisfied with the answers.

Last year, the fourteen-year-old mixed-breed dog of one of my neighbors was put on steroids and cortisone in order to treat its serious case of arthritis. I was very concerned about possible side effects from the level of drugs in the dog's system and suggested the man look into an alternative solution for his dog. Cortisone causes the bones to become frail and brittle, even while it is working to offset inflammation and pain. In the long run it can actually do more damage than help for an older dog.

My neighbor found a new vet who took his dog off steroids and put it on B_{12} injections instead to reduce the inflammation. He decided to add yucca and cartilage supplements to the dog's food. Soon his dog was walking around wonderfully, without much pain and stiffness. The last time I spoke with him he told me, "If I had only known earlier, I could have saved my dog a lot of discomfort."

My client's first veterinarian had not been open-minded enough to investigate natural supplements and vitamin therapy. But if the second veterinarian knew this treatment, why couldn't the first vet learn it or find out?

Nutrition is a component of treatment for the vast majority of physical conditions and ailments your dog will face during its lifetime, and holistic veterinary care is the context for the return to the natural, whole-food diet that I advocate. Simply put, the basic idea is to prevent disease by not contributing to it in the first place.

The good news is that you can learn to promote your dog's health through homemade meals that may easily be prepared in your own kitchen. The recipes I cook at Barker's Grub that are found in this book are derived from my old family recipes and my imagination. It is written for you, the reader, who wishes to give your beloved dogs the absolute best possible care and ensure them health and happiness. The feeding instructions are straightforward and based on sound nutritional principles and practices. I hope it inspires you to take action.

Chapter 1

What's Wrong with Processed Dog Food?

Why would you ever feed your dog something you would not feed your children or eat yourself? Think about it. For that is what you are doing when you are feeding your pet from cans of processed dog food and bags of dry rations. If you look at it closely, this practice defies common sense. There have been many books and articles written in recent years attacking the dog food industry, but that is not my primary goal in this book. I am concerned only with how to achieve optimal nutrition found through the benefits of whole food. A dog that is consuming processed foods cannot possibly attain peak physical and mental potential simply because peak nutritional values are not being obtained. In this chapter, we will explore some of the reasons this is true.

DANGEROUS PRESERVATIVES

Processed food is less fresh than food that is specially prepared at home and eaten shortly after cooking. Any food product that goes into a can or bag to be sold off the shelf in a store must be preserved, and the wholesomeness of such products should be called into question. If there is no expiration date on the label, the product may be past its prime. If it is chemically preserved, you have to wonder about how safe those chemicals are. That is why it is much better to cook at home and make fresh food.

Homemade dog food can be prepared ahead and frozen for the week to come.

Preservatives can build up in the body over time and pollute the digestive system, thereby interfering with the normal functions of organs that maintain good health and cleanse the body, such as the liver and kidneys. This buildup happens faster in smaller animals than humans. Chemicals such as Ethoxyquin, BHA, and BHT are commonplace preservatives, and independent laboratory research has shown all three to be suspected carcinogens. Other probable hazards include liver damage, fetal abnormalities, and thyroid dysfunction.

QUESTIONABLE INGREDIENTS

Who knows what is in processed food? You never have to wonder if you make your dog's meals yourself, since you can eliminate unwanted—even harmful—ingredients from your dog's diet. When reading the labels on brand-name dog food containers, you'll find it is not always easy to identify the ingredients mentioned. What is a meat by-product or a chicken by-product? What about animal digest? These are euphemisms for ingredients that would not sound so healthy called by their right names. Pet food companies are not obliged to list all the ingredients that go into their products, and oftentimes the ingredients listed on the labels go by names that the ordinary consumer cannot recognize.

The pet food industry is not regulated by the government in the same way as the Food and Drug Administration (FDA) regulates food designated for human beings. The industry has a self-regulatory board, the American Association of Feed Control Officials (AAFCO), which defines the nutritional, testing, and labeling requirements for processed dog food. See the "crude analysis" section on any label. What you will read there is a breakdown of percentages for protein, fat, fiber, certain minerals, and so forth. The labels do list ingredients—in descending order from greatest to least by weight—although they do not list the exact percentages that contribute to the crude analysis of nutritional values. In other words, is the protein source from meat or something else? Is the calcium source bone meal or eggshells?

Even more frightening, the feed eaten by the chickens or cattle that go into the dog food—and human food—may be contaminated by chemicals. For example, *The Agribusiness Examiner*, a public interest magazine, reported in September 1999 that U.S. poultry producers are using a chemical called polyacrylamide to extract proteins, fats, and other nutrients from wastewater at their plants by reducing it to a sludge that is then added to animal feed. Sludge-fed meat can find its way into your dog's food (and your own). The U.S. Environmental Protection Agency has classified polyacrylamide as a carcinogen, and the FDA has not approved it for use, although that agency appears to turn a blind eye, since the practice just described occurs.

BULK INGREDIENTS

Processed dog foods consist of over 50 percent bulk ingredients, some as much as 75 percent. Bulk ingredient is any ingredient besides meat; usually it is a carbohydrate. The bulk ingredient may consist of wheat, corn, and soy. In most cases, the rest of bulk ingredients are meat by-products, which are not really the meat but ground-up parts of the animal (intestines, spleen, feet, lungs and the like). Through my business as a dog food chef, I have often encountered dogs that have very bad flatulence. This excess gas is caused by poor nutrition and indigestion, soy products being a major culprit. Obviously the dogs are having a hard time digesting all the bulk ingredients in their overly processed and synthetic dog foods, because the problem disappears after they go on a home-cooked diet.

Since domestic dogs are descendants of wild dogs, we can look to contemporary African wild dogs and other wild canids like wolves and coyotes for clues as to what should be in dog food. It is fair to assume that its wild ancestors influenced your dog's genetics. A dog's natural diet would never contain synthetic minerals and other supplements, and would not include corn and other fillers. Instead, it would consist of raw meat, bones, and some roots, herbs, and vegetables. There are many benefits to such a diet. First, as dogs in the wild do not have access to many carbohydrates, they do not get fat.

In addition, raw food may strengthen the immune system. In "Treating Heartworm Holistically" (*Whole Dog Journal,* June 1998), Nancy Kerns reported on her interview with Dr. William Falconer, a homeopathic veterinarian from Austin, Texas. Dr. Falconer says that dogs need a natural diet and lifestyle and that with minimal vaccinations and curtailed exposure to flea-killing pesticides, domestic dogs should be better able to fend off parasitic diseases such as heartworm. Parasites have evolved in such a way that they don't kill their hosts. Wolves and coyotes, which, like dogs, are members of the canine family, are exposed to heartworm in the wild, but their immune systems are better able to fight it off. On the other hand, domestic dogs that get heartworm can die from it. Furthermore, they require treatment with poisonous substances that often have negative side effects. While it is not the only weak link in the standard chain of dog health, a processed-food diet lacks the immune-boosting punch of a natural diet.

Mysterious Processes

Lastly, the pet food industry is a big, highly competitive, and hugely profitable business; therefore, dog food companies keep their recipes and preparation processes closely guarded secrets. Because we don't know exactly what the pet food companies do to process their dog foods, we can only trust that they do not overcook it to rob it of essential nutrients. When foods are over-cooked, which might be done to sterilize their contents, for example, they lose much of their nutritional value. The minerals are processed out of them, so then they have to be artificially supplemented. Many of the ingredients on pet food labels are synthetic nutrients added back into the processed food.

To be fair, according to Dr. Michael Fox, author of *Understanding Your Dog* and an expert on animal care and proponent of animal rights, the commercial dog food industry has become more responsive to the legitimate concerns and health problems that have arisen from dogs being fed certain commercial diets. As a result, a new generation of higher quality dog foods is now being marketed. Nonetheless, he states, "Most are still convenience foods, the ingredients of which have been subjected to various food processing procedures, including high temperatures and various methods of storage, preserving, and packaging such that the final product may not have the same nutritional value as the label indicates."

Processed dog foods now are also marketed toward categories such as seniors, puppies, and for management of specific ailments. No matter what is on the label, however, proper nutrition is a highly individualized balance of requirements dictated by genetics, age, health status, and activity. A good veterinarian should ask about your dog's response to what it is eating. Of course, dog food manufacturers do conduct feeding and digestibility research trials, but the bottom line is that one kind of dog food is not going to be good for all dogs.

DRY FOOD

In my opinion, the scourge of sound dog nutrition is most processed dry food, especially when that is all the dog gets to eat. The biggest problem with dry food is that it is dehydrated, so it robs dogs of water. An extreme example of what might go wrong is the case I once heard of a five-year-old dog that had been on a dry-food-only diet all its life. This dog suddenly developed symptoms of vomiting and diarrhea, and it had blood in its stools. The veterinarian treating the dog ultimately had to operate. It turned out that the unhappy dog had an ulcer in its intestines, which its dry food was exacerbating. Some food was even stuck to the lining of the intestine. I believe that if this dog's food had been moister, it may have passed through its body more easily, and its symptoms would have been lessened.

A common myth about dry food is that it cleans your dog's teeth. In fact, it does not because it crumbles and breaks apart. What really works for teeth cleaning is the raw food that canine animals eat in the wild. Raw meat contains a high percentage of blood and other bodily fluids that hydrate the dog, and while the flesh and bones get chewed and worked up and around the dog's teeth and gums, they also eliminate plaque and bacteria.

Depending on the brand, dry food may also contain a lot of sodium, probably for flavor, and that can make your dog drink to excess. Even if you leave a bowl of fresh water out for your dog while it is eating, it may not be drinking enough. If your dog is diabetic, you will have to carefully monitor its salt intake. Dry food can create a behavioral problem, too, because any dog that is home alone with a constant source of dry food must drink a lot to accommodate the salt in its intake. Eventually the dog will have to relieve itself—possibly on your favorite carpet!

Dog Treats

Dog biscuits, or cookies as I call them, are essentially composed of carbohydrates and other ingredients that can make your dog fat. They should not be substituted for regular food, and should be given to your dog only in moderation. Otherwise, cookies are okay for dogs as long as they do not contain preservatives.

It is also fine to give your dog beef jerky or a meat-based treat it loves if the treat has no preservatives besides salt—but even jerky should be given in moderation. The truth is that, on an emotional basis, treats are completely unnecessary because dogs will generally do as much for your praise as they will for their food.

One more important matter is the rawhide chews. These are made of skin and are loaded with an enormous amount of chemicals, like formaldehyde, bleaches, and synthesized flavors (all of which are synthetic chemicals). Avoid them at all costs. For certain, the chew treats such as pigs ears have also been chemically processed. Cow hooves may have been treated with preservatives as well. Better to get a nice beef bone for Fido from the butcher.

In recent years, the general public and the medical establishment have begun to accept that—for human beings—nutrition is one of the most powerful tools we have available to create optimal health for ourselves. It is the cornerstone of preventive care and healing. Adages have honored this truth for centuries: an apple a day keeps the doctor away. Today, many dog lovers are beginning to apply the same holistic approach to pet nutrition. Why not? It is such a simple solution.

Advocates of the traditional philosophy recognize that the true benefits of feeding your dog processed foods, such as speed and convenience—and the more mythical benefits, such as "scientifically formulated" recipes for complete nutrition—are far outweighed by the detriments that the processing of dog food poses to your pet's health in the long term. In the next chapter, we will take a look at the advantages of home-cooking dog food.

Barker's Grub

Chapter 2

What Dog Food Should Be

Quality food means quality life. Along with regular veterinary visits, keeping our companion animals happy, and abundant exercise, there is no other single aspect of pet care that is so vital to well-being throughout the course of our dogs' lives. Paramount to good canine health is a balanced and wholesome diet.

Commercial dog food originated in the late nineteenth century but did not become popular until the 1920s. Until that time, dogs ate what humans ate. Older generations still remember preparing meals for their pets. Then, as people became busier with everyday life, or were working longer hours, we lost sight of how little time it really takes—and how important it really is—to cook for our companion animals and ourselves. New technology and the demand of the marketplace supported the transformation. We opted, as a society, for convenience in a can. We seem to have lost the commonsense knowledge behind the nature of ingredients and the role of food in the lifestyle.

For many years, I was a perfect illustration of the dog food dilemma. I only knew how to boil water and make eggs, and I did not even have confidence enough to prepare noodles because I thought I was doing them "wrong." I was afraid to go near the vegetables in the grocery store because cooking them would be "like brain surgery." Because I had never learned how to cook for myself, I could not cook for my dog.

What is odd is that I grew up in a home where my mother cooked constantly and emphasized the importance of nutrition to my brother and me. Likewise, my grandmother, who had raised six children on home cooking, would come to visit and cook. She possessed Old World knowledge about the health benefits of every vegetable, fruit, and meat. Nonetheless, when I grew up and left the nest, I ate very poorly. I didn't learn until necessity forced me to change.

What, then, is dog food? Let us take all the mystery out of the subject. Dog food should follow the rules of commonsense nutrition. I am amazed at some of the claims made for the magical properties of commercial food. Dogs and humans have lived together as companions for so many tens of thousands of years that our basic nutritional needs are similar. That is why there is no need for your dog's meals to be more—or less—than simple, wholesome ingredients from the grocery store, prepared at home according to sensible, straightforward instructions. Dog food is food that you and I are also able to consume. Nothing fancy.

Proper nutrition is essential to a healthier, happier—and longer—life for your dog. However, the nutritional needs of dogs vary according to their age, breed, stresses, and health status. These can best be monitored in the home environment and by feeding the dog a homemade diet, the ingredients and quantities of which can be fine-tuned by the owner in collaboration with a vet or nutritional expert throughout the dog's life.

BENEFITS OF HOME COOKING

Before we move to a discussion of the independent factors that must be considered in planning your dog's diet, let us take a look at the overall picture. There are many significant benefits to feeding your dog homemade dog food. These are both physical and emotional, and they impact on your dog's health as well as your own:

- Every dog is an individual and should be treated that way. By cooking for your dog, you can effectively control what your pet eats and make certain that it receives only the most wholesome food, and a balanced diet designed with your dog's unique nutritional needs in mind.

- Food sharing is important to your dog's emotional well-being. One of the reasons dogs get along so well with us is that we can form tribes together. In the wild, dogs form packs and share the carcasses of the animals they hunt. Wildlife biologists have documented cases of African wild dogs in which one dog coming back from the hunt will regurgitate a piece of meat for another dog. That dog will then regurgitate some meat for another dog. Every dog in a pack will make food available this way for any pup in the group.

  In captivity, adult wolves have been observed to act like cubs by licking the pack leader's mouth, prompting the leader, the alpha male, to regurgitate food for them. Animal expert Dr. Michael Fox interprets this as a ritual display indicating that the pack leader is also a kind of parent figure. Human beings are also social and altruistic animals by nature. The ideal human-dog relationship is one in which the human being is not simply a domineering alpha but a caregiving parent figure and a playmate.

- When you are home-cooking meals and feeding your dogs, it makes them more willing to cooperate in their own training. Dogs appreciate the care and attention you give them and feel your love, and they respond to it with loyalty. Dogs share with us the ability to empathize, to be able to sense what their packmates and human companions are feeling. You and your dog can develop a deep and satisfying understanding of each other—a more soulful connection—in the process. Dogs want to please you.

• Sound nutrition is the cornerstone of preventive medicine. Many diseases can be prevented if proper nutrition is begun early in the dog's life. A poor diet, conversely, can lead to immune-system disorders, thus making your pet more prone to diseases and even certain allergies. According to holistic veterinarian Monique Maniet of Veterinary Holistic Care of Bethesda, Maryland, 99 percent of ailments are linked to nutritional deficiencies and all should be treated with nutritional means, as well as other medical therapies.

• The joy and companionship of dogs promotes mental and physical health in humans. A study of pet therapy on senior citizens in nursing homes, for example, revealed that otherwise unresponsive geriatric patients would respond to four-legged creatures. In a study of patients undergoing physical therapy for muscular conditions, those who were in contact with dogs made a bigger effort to move, probably to keep up. Research has also shown that petting an animal lowers blood pressure and reduces people's susceptibility to heart attacks.

• As you cook for your pet, your own nutrition and eating habits will improve. Time and time again I have witnessed this with my clients and friends. As they realize how easy cooking actually is—and how much pleasure it can bring—as well as the astonishing physical benefits of good nutrition, they start modifying what they eat for the better.

- You will save money. A healthy animal means fewer visits to the veterinarian. Home cooking is economical as well as nutritious.

How can you determine the right balance of food for your dog? A good place to start is by considering genetics.

BREED VARIATIONS

Like human beings, dogs are omnivores; they eat every kind of food including meat, vegetables, and grains. A dog needs protein, fat, carbohydrates, and minerals. By extension, you could say that the most basic nutritional requirement for dogs is to eat a diet properly balanced among these many diverse foods. (Chapter 3 provides more details on each of these food components.) However, different breeds of dog do well or poorly on certain ingredients. After all, any food that is not digestible to a certain animal or breed will not nourish it.

A key consideration when planning a menu is bioavailability. It is important to know whether a dog can or cannot absorb nutrients from a specific ingredient. No matter if your dog is a pure breed or a mixed-heritage dog—a *Natural* Dog—the environment of its ancestors dictates the foods that are best for it. Dogs evolved in harmony with their surroundings over many thousands of years, and these origins are imbedded in dogs' genetic makeup.

An insightful book by William D. Cusick, *Canine Nutrition*, explores the impact of regional origins on canine nutrition. He postulates, for example, that a breed that comes from a region on the seacoast may do better on saltwater fish than a breed cultivated in a freshwater area, although both saltwater and freshwater fishes contain essential omega-3 fatty acids. A breed from the tropics, such as the Chihuahua, may need vitamins and minerals that are bioavailable in tropical fruit, like the avocado or mango. A breed that evolved in the tundra, such as the Siberian Husky, needs a diet composed of high fat and protein that would have enabled it to survive in a cold climate. The idea seems sound (and I have adopted the basic premise in my cooking), if, while looking as far back in a dog's origins as possible, you can find a way to translate its genetic requirements into contemporary and readily available ingredients.

Genetic predispositions also exist to specific physical ailments, like hip dysplasia and epilepsy. We can see these conditions running in breeds. In many cases, these are modern predispositions created by the practice of overbreeding for specific traits. Sometimes there are nutritional coping strategies for inbred ailments, sometimes not.

It is unlikely that you can do grave harm in the short term to your pet. While the region from which a breed originates may contribute to your dog's individual dietary profile, a given dog is not going to distinguish or discriminate between one food and another when he or she is hungry. In the wild, it would be more likely that a dog would come across an animal carcass or root and eat it, and if the food disagreed with his stomach he would simply vomit it up or avoid such food next time.

The following breed list is organized by size first and breed second. It notes the recorded place of origin and the type of work for which the breed was cultivated and used, in addition to its optimal food sources and genetic proclivities—when they are known. Many breeds are so ancient that their true origins have been lost.

The foodstuffs I have indicated are only samples of ingredients your dog may be predisposed to eat. Do not forget that dogs must be fed a wide variety of foods. You will understand more about this last consideration when you come to the feeding instructions and recipes in Chapters 5 and 6. These breed profiles are useful guideposts for what your dog may most need and do well eating; nonetheless they are not written in stone, and you should follow common sense and the advice of your veterinarian to determine what your pet's unique needs are.

The Natural Dog (All Weights and Sizes)

Natural Dog

Mixed Origin. Size range: variable. Natural Dogs have done every job imaginable, including giving love and companionship. If you know some of a Natural Dog's heritage you can cross-check those mixed breeds for clues about dietary needs. For the most part, natural dogs should eat every kind of food—lamb, poultry, beef, fish, wheat, rice, barley, oats, green vegetables, and tubers or roots like sweet potato, and potato, for starters.

More than one research study has shown that the healthiest and least problem-ridden dogs in the world are the mongrels or mixed breeds. In fact, if purebred dogs were to breed independently of human intervention they would, within two or three generations, come to resemble the Pariah Dog that exists everywhere on the earth, from Mexico to India, Australia, and the Middle East. (The only place where it is said that dogs did not exist indigenously is Iceland.) My dog Oscar is a prime specimen of this Natural Dog.

You could say that pure breeds are actually dogs that have been selected for their *recessive* genetic traits. The *dominant* characteristics of the canine species will come out whenever dogs mix freely. If you have no bias toward a specific breed based on its appearance, Natural Dogs make great companions and will have fewer physical ailments than others. You can find them in shelters or on the streets of any town or city in America. I am a major advocate of the Natural Dog.

Small Dogs (Up to 35 Pounds)

American Cocker Spaniel

Spain. Size range: 20–27 pounds. A bird dog. Cocker Spaniels need higher amino acids, extra taurine, and more vitamin A than most dogs. They do well on wheat, poultry, and dairy.

Basenji

Central Africa. Size range: 23–25 pounds. A sight hunter for partridge and rabbit. Basenjis should eat beef, poultry, wheat, and brown or white rice.

Beagle

England. Size range: 20–30 pounds. A hunting dog. They require a diet high in fats and carbohydrates. Beagles should eat beets, potato, wheat, lamb, rabbit, and poultry.

Bichon Frise

Mediterranean France and Italy. Size range: 11–15 pounds. An ornamental sea dog. They need a high-fat diet with sulfates and limestone. They develop kidney stones when dietary minerals are from other sources they cannot assimilate. Bichon Frises need fish, wheat, rice, green vegetables, poultry, lamb, and avocado.

Cairn Terrier

Coastal Scotland. Size range: 12–15 pounds. A vermin hunter. Cairn Terriers should eat fish, poultry, and wheat.

Cardigan Welsh Corgi

Welsh Highlands. Size range: 33–35 pounds. A hunter and cattle herder. They need a lot of calcium, phosphorus, and iodine. Corgis do well on rye, cabbage, potato, carrots, beef, rabbit, fish, and oats.

Chihuahua

Mexico. Size range: 4–6 pounds. A rodent hunter. They especially need tropical fruits. The best food for Chihuahuas includes mango, avocado, poultry, and rice.

Dachshund

Germany. Size range: 16–22 pounds. A rodent hunter. They need lots of vitamin A, high fat, and low protein. Dachshunds should eat potato, cabbage, carrots, green vegetables, wheat, and beef.

Jack Russell Terrier

Southern England. Size range: 13–17 pounds. A fox-hunting dog. Jack Russells can eat poultry, potato, sweet potato, dairy, wheat, beets, beef, and lamb.

Lhasa Apso

Himalayas, Tibet. Size range: 16–18 pounds. An ornamental temple dog. They require high fat and do well on lamb, goat, poultry, fish, rice, and wheat.

Pug

Lowlands, Tibet. Size range: 14–18 pounds. An ornamental dog. They need a high fat-to-protein ratio in their diet. Pugs should have barley, beef, and rye.

Scottish Terrier

Highlands, Scotland. Size range: 18–22 pounds. A hare and rodent hunter. Scottish Terriers would do well on lamb, poultry, dairy, beef, green vegetables, potato, wheat, and barley.

Shih-Tzu

Tibet. Size range: 12–15 pounds. An ornamental and watch-dog. They need a diet high in fat and low in protein. Shih-Tzus might eat poultry, pork, barley, rice, and wheat.

Yorkshire Terrier

England. Size range: 5–7 pounds. A rodent hunter. Yorkshire Terriers thrive on dairy, beef, lamb, potato, beets, rye, and barley.

Medium Dogs (35–60 Pounds)

Afghan Hound

Afghanistan/Ancient Egypt. Size range: 50–60 pounds. A sight hound for hunting antelope, hare, mountain deer, and wolves. They need high fiber and high carbohydrates. These dogs have sensitivity to pesticides. Foods that Afghan Hounds should eat include poultry, lamb, brown rice, and wheat.

Airedale Terrier

Yorkshire County, England. Size range: 45–60 pounds. A hunting and water dog. They require a higher amount of fatty acids than most dogs; otherwise they tend to get a very dry coat and "hot spots," red, inflamed itchy areas on their skin. Normally, they would have eaten a lot of freshwater fish. Food that Airedale Terriers need includes beef, venison, freshwater fish, carrots, potatoes, cabbage, wheat, and oats.

Basset Hound

France. Size range: 40–50. A small-game hunting dog. They need high fiber and high carbohydrates. Foods Basset Hounds do well on are venison, rabbit, poultry, lamb, wheat, and beets.

Border Collie

Scotland. Size range: 35–55 pounds. A shepherd dog. They need a diet high in fat and carbohydrates. Border Collies should eat potato, wheat, lamb, fish, and poultry.

Bulldog

Northern England. Size range: 40–50 pounds. A blood-sport dog. They need high carbohydrates. Bulldogs do well on beef, dairy, wheat, potato, and cabbage.

Canaan Dog

Israel. Size range: 35–55 pounds. A herding and flock-guarding dog. Canaan Dogs should do well on wheat, lamb, and poultry.

Chinese Shar-Pei

Southern China. Size range: 45–60 pounds. An ornamental dog. They need high fiber and high carbohydrates in their diet. Chinese Shar-Peis do well on poultry, wheat, rice, beets, potato, pork, and beef.

English Springer Spaniel

England. Size range: 44–55 pounds. A hunting dog. They need a high-fat diet that includes wheat, lamb, and poultry.

Field Spaniel

Spain. Size range: 35–50 pounds. A bird hunter. They need a high-fat diet that includes wheat, oats, lamb, and poultry.

Greyhound

Egypt. Size range: 60–75 pounds. A hunting dog. This ancient breed particularly needs vitamins A, D, and E, and trace minerals, such as selenium. They need a low-fat and high-protein diet. Greyhounds would do well on poultry, lamb, dried fruits (such as figs and raisins), nuts (such as walnuts and almonds), barley, wheat, and brown or white rice.

Keeshond

Holland. Size range: 35–40 pounds. A watchdog and hunter. They need high protein, low carbohydrates, and extra flaxseed oil. Keeshonds should eat fish, dairy, rice, beets, and poultry.

Pit Bull Terrier

Florida, United States. Size range: 24–38 pounds. They need high fiber and high fat content in their diet. Pit Bulls do well on cabbage, potato, carrots, white or brown rice, venison, fish, beef, and poultry.

Shibainu

Japan. Size range: 30–40 pounds. A small-game hunter. Shibainus should eat sweet potato, green vegetables, cabbage, rice, poultry, lamb, and fish.

Standard Poodle

France. Size range: 45–65 pounds. A water dog. They need a diet high in both the amino acid phenylanyline and in minerals. It affects their coat and skin if these come from the wrong source (both the skin and fur begin to turn orange). Poodles should eat fish, poultry, pork, wheat, barley, and white or brown rice.

Standard Schnauzer

Germany. Size range: 30–50 pounds. A herding and guard dog. Standard Schnauzers should eat carrots, cabbage, rye, potato, pork, beef, and lamb.

Vizsla

Hungary. Size range: 45–50 pounds. A water dog. They need a high-fiber diet from wheat, barley, rye, oats, beef, pork, lamb, and poultry.

Large Dogs (60–90 Pounds)

Akita

Gifu, Nagano, and Toyama, Japan. Size range: 75–100 pounds. A hunting dog for tracking boar and deer. In the Akita diet, the meat should be fatty, and they require higher carbohydrates. They do well on venison, fish, poultry, rice, green beans, cabbage, sweet potato, and wheat.

Alaskan Malamute

Alaska, United States. Size range: 70–85. A guard dog, tracking dog, and sled dog that originates from an extremely cold region. Malamutes need extra fatty acids in their diet, which can come from flaxseed oil or salmon oil. Their diet should include saltwater and freshwater fish, such as salmon, tilapia, and flounder, as well as poultry, lamb, and rice.

Borzoi

Russia. Size range: 60–105 pounds. A wolf hunter. They need high fiber and do well on wheat, alfalfa, and beef.

Boxer

Germany. Size range: 60–70 pounds. A guard dog. Their diet should include high levels of fat and fiber, and trace minerals. A boxer's pancreas produces digestive enzymes at a rate that makes them prone to excess gas and indigestion. They should eat foods such as oats, rye, pork, and poultry.

Chesapeake Bay Retriever

Maryland, United States. Size range: 55–75 pounds. A hunting and water dog. They need extra fatty acids from flaxseed oil and fish oil for their coat, which produces an oil. Feed them fish, duck, poultry, rice, and wheat.

Chow Chow

China. Size range: 60–70. A human food source. They should eat high-fiber diets. Chow Chows do well on rice, wheat, and fish.

Collie

Scotland. Size range: 50–75 pounds. A herding dog. Collies need more vitamin D than other dogs, so you should supplement them carefully. They thrive on green vegetables, lamb, poultry, and beef.

Dalmatian

Eastern Europe. Size range: 45–65 pounds. A war and guard dog. Dalmatians should eat lamb, poultry, and white rice and no organ meats. Dalmatians are prone to forming urate bladder stones, so they need low purine in their diet.

German Shepherd

Germany. Size range: 65–85 pounds. A shepherding and tracking dog. They have an exceptionally short colon and therefore need a diet high in fiber to aid digestion. German Shepherds do well when fed beef, wheat, leafy greens, cabbage, alfalfa, and lamb.

Golden Retriever

Unknown Origin. Size range: 60–75 pounds. A hunting and water dog. Fatty acids are important for the skin and coat. Golden Retrievers should receive a diet of beef, poultry, fish, potato, and wheat.

Irish Setter

Ireland. Size range: 60–70 pounds. A bird dog. They need high fat and high carbohydrates. Irish Setters should eat green vegetables, fish, poultry, potato, carrots, rye, and lamb.

Labrador Retriever

England. Size range: 55–75 pounds. A bird and water dog. This breed needs extra fatty acids for its coat, as well as high fat and low carbohydrates. Labrador Retrievers do well when fed fish, poultry, lamb, dairy, wheat, olive oil, and green vegetables.

Old English Sheepdog

England. Size range: 75–90 pounds. A shepherding dog. They need a low-fat diet. Old English Sheepdogs should thrive on lamb, beef, wheat, oats, beets, potato, and green vegetables.

Rhodesian Ridgeback

Southern Africa. Size range: 65–75 pounds. A lion fighter and hunter. Rhodesian Ridgebacks should eat ground nuts (such as peanuts, almonds, and walnuts), lamb, poultry, wheat, and white or brown rice.

Samoyed

Finland. Size range: 40–75 pounds. A reindeer herder and cart dog. They require a diet high in fat and carbohydrates. Feed them fish, potato, wheat, and poultry.

Weimaraner

Germany. Size range: 55–85 pounds (females are often much smaller than males). A wild-game hunter. They need high-fat food. You may give them potato, cabbage, alfalfa, barley, pork, poultry, beef, and lamb.

Giant Dogs (90 Pounds and Above)

Bernese Mountain Dog

Swiss Alps. Size range: 75–105 pounds. A livestock herding and cart dog. Due to the high mineral content in the soil of the Bern region, this breed developed a need for a unique balance of minerals such as selenium, zinc, iron, and manganese. These are all metals found in lime soil. They also need a high-fat diet. Bernese Mountain Dogs do well on wheat, greens, lamb, and poultry.

Great Dane

Ancient Rome. Size range: 120–150 pounds. A guard dog, hunter, and war dog. They require high protein. Feed them oats, cabbage, rye, potato, and beef.

Great Pyrenees

France. Size range: 90–125 pounds. A shepherd dog. They need a high fat-to-protein ratio. Great Pyrenees can eat any grains and vegetables. Feed them wheat, potato, lamb, and poultry.

Irish Wolfhound
Ancient Rome. Size range: 105–120 pounds. A war dog and elk hunter. They need high carbohydrate, high fiber, and low protein. Irish Wolfhounds should eat wheat, barley, potato, beef, and lamb.

Rottweiler
Northern Italy. Size range: 100–115 pounds. They have a more extended puppyhood than most dogs, so they need a high-protein diet for the first two and a half years of life. Grown Rottweilers need a diet high in carbohydrates and fat. Feed them dairy, lamb, poultry, fish, roots, wheat, rice, and barley.

Scottish Deerhound
Ancient Egypt. Size range: 75–110 pounds (females are often much smaller than males). A hunting dog. These dogs benefit from extra fatty acids, which they can get from flaxseed oil. Scottish Deerhounds should do well on lamb, poultry, rice, wheat, and potato.

St. Bernard
Switzerland. Size range: 145–165 pounds. A rescue and cart dog. St. Bernards should eat dairy, wheat, lamb, poultry, roots, and green vegetables.

ASSESSING YOUR DOG'S NUTRITIONAL NEEDS

This simple worksheet is designed to help you profile your dog so that you and the veterinarian can come up with an eating plan. It may give you ideas for points to bring up during an office visit. Also see the "Special Cases" chapter (Chapter 4) when designing a diet for your dog.

Age:

Size (height and weight):

Breed:

Health History (prebirth to the present):

Medications:

Disposition (e.g., calm or nervous):

Exercise (e.g., frequent or infrequent):

Emotional Stress Factors (e.g., transitions and loss):

Environmental Conditions (e.g., climate and crowding):

In the next chapter, we will explore the specific nutrients that dogs require, as well as the whole-food sources where they can be found.

Chapter 3

Canine Nutrients

Vitamins, Minerals, and Supplements Your Dog Needs

Nourishment for dogs, just like human beings, must always be drawn from a broad range of foods that contain macronutrients (protein, carbohydrates—including fiber—and fat), micronutrients (vitamins and minerals), and water. Each of these is a key component of the canine diet, and there are natural ways of introducing them into your dog's meals. In this chapter, we will look at what characterizes good overall nutrition, the whole-food sources of specific nutrients, and the hidden potential deficits in food values, as well as what supplements to use—and when—to ensure that appropriate nutritional values are being met.

Dogs' nutritional and caloric requirements will differ according to their breed, age, and health status, hence the need for us to pay close attention. You may be surprised what you will pick up when you become aware of subtle changes in your dog's behavior and appearance. A dog can best be monitored in the home environment throughout its life cycle by feeding it a homemade diet. In collaboration with a veterinarian or nutritional expert, the essential ingredients and quantities can be fine-tuned by the owner.

These days, dogs suffer few severe nutritional deficiencies because people are feeding them better (processed foods are included in this assessment). It is rare, for example, to see a puppy with rickets, a painful condition caused by calcium and vitamin D deficiency in which the bones become softened and weakened. It is also rare to observe a dog with black tongue, also known as pellagra, a condition caused by a deficiency of niacin. Remember, prior to the twentieth century, dogs typically consumed the same food their owners did or ate their owners' unwanted scraps. Dogs used to suffer and die from black tongue, as did thousands of people, when their diets, which usually consisted of too much salt pork, corn, and potatoes, didn't have enough variety to give them the nutrients they needed.

Not all nutrient deficiencies are so extreme; nonetheless, the importance of feeding your dog a balanced diet cannot be overemphasized. Many physical and psychological ailments are a direct result of insufficient trace minerals. Epilepsy, for example, can be the direct result of magnesium deficiency. Similarly, a diet low in fat may trigger aggression. Meals, and an ongoing menu, composed of diverse ingredients are the only means to ensure the full complement of essential nutrients.

What, then, are the necessary components of a dog's diet? Where do they come from and why does the body need them? How does cooking impact their value to the body? Let us first look at the large scale, the macronutrients.

MACRONUTRIENTS

Foods that must be eaten in large quantities are called macronutrients. *Macro* means "big." The macronutrients are protein, carbohydrates, and fat. They have been called the building blocks of life. During digestion, enzymes in the juices of the stomach and intestines chemically dissolve foods, thus making it possible for the body to absorb and use the available nutrients. The macronutrients participate in and fuel numerous metabolic functions that keep dogs alive and healthy.

Protein

Dogs must eat more protein than any other type of food. Protein supplies amino acids, which are the infrastructure of the body. It is used to build and maintain muscle mass, and helps regulate hormones and brain chemicals. If a dog does not eat enough protein, its body begins to take protein from the existing lean muscle mass, weakening the animal. There are two types of protein: complete proteins and combined proteins.

Protein is composed of bonds of twenty-two amino acids in various combinations. Some of these amino acids are manufactured within a dog's body, so they do not have to be ingested. Some must be taken from food. The second kind are called essential amino acids and include valine, leucine, isoleucine, threonine, methionine, phenylalanine, tryptophan, histidine, arginine, and lysine. The quality of a protein is directly related to the number and amount of essential amino acids it contains.

Complete proteins are those foods that supply all the essential amino acids in sufficient amounts. These are found in eggs, meat, fish, and dairy products such as milk and cheese. Soy is the only plant-based complete protein. I do not advocate feeding soy to most dogs, because it would not be available to them in the wild and therefore their bodies are not genetically predisposed to digest it.

Incomplete proteins are foods that are missing several amino acids. Sources of incomplete proteins include legumes, whole grains, nuts, and seeds. To satisfy the body's need for amino acids, these must be eaten in combination with others. When two or more plant-based proteins are eaten in combination, they can create a complete protein. For example, rice and beans create a complete protein. Cereals such as oats and barley are very low in amino acids.

When protein is cooked, it becomes less digestible. It loses natural enzymes when exposed to heat. Think of the toughness of beef jerky. On the other hand, a raw steak left sitting on a plate begins to break down from its own internal juices. Cooked protein lasts longer than uncooked protein because heat acts as a preservative.

WHOLE-FOOD SOURCES OF AMINO ACIDS

Beef	*Pork*
Cheese	*Lamb*
Chicken	*Milk*
Cottage cheese	*Oats*
Eggs	*Tuna*
Nuts	*Turkey*
Fish	*Wheat germ*
Leafy green vegetables	*Yogurt*

Carbohydrates

All vegetables, fruits, cereals, and grains contain carbohydrates. Carbohydrates include everything that isn't fat or protein or water. They supply the dog's body with instant energy. Although protein and fat provide sustained energy, those are sources of reserved calories locked into muscles and organs. Surplus carbohydrates are generally stored as fat for the body's future use in cases of famine, which is why an overfed dog grows obese.

There are two types of carbohydrates: simple and complex.

Simple carbohydrates include table sugar (sucrose)—which your dog does not need—fruit sugar (fructose), and milk sugar (lactose). Fruit provides fiber, vitamins, and minerals, along with energy. Milk provides protein and fat along with energy. Starchy vegetables or roots, such as potato, sweet potato, carrots, turnips, and beets, contain simple carbohydrates in combination with other essential nutrients.

Complex carbohydrates are composed of longer strands of sugar molecules and come from vegetables, legumes (beans, lentils, and peas), and whole grains, such as wheat and barley. Complex carbohydrates are the most ideal carbohydrates to consume because they metabolize quickly, and contain essential nutrients.

Unlike protein, the more you cook carbohydrates, the easier they become to digest. Think about how a stalk of broccoli becomes softer when cooked. The danger, of course, is that you might cook vegetables and other carbohydrates for so long that the other essential nutrients get lost in the process.

For most of this book, "carbohydrates" will refer to grains and starchy vegetables, while "vegetables" will refer to other vegetables.

Fiber

Even though the dog cannot digest fiber, fiber is a key component of the diet. A dog needs fiber to slow the movement of food through the digestive tract, giving it enough time to absorb the essential nutrients in the food. Vitamin K is produced inside a dog when the resident bacteria in the gut interact with fiber. Dietary fiber alleviates both diarrhea and constipation. It creates bulk in the stools because it has a water-containing capacity, and that bulk signals the body to maintain proper bowel function. It can inhibit fat absorption and increase the excretion of cholesterol. Fiber binds with toxins and wastes, and helps neutralize them before they do damage to the body. Fiber is truly significant.

Fiber is found almost exclusively in plant foods—vegetables, fruit, legumes, whole grains, nuts, and seeds. There are two categories of fiber: insoluble (also called roughage) and soluble. Insoluble fiber, such as cellulose, is found in the skins and stalks of fruits and vegetables, wheat bran, peanut shells and cereals. It is not digestible and contains no available nutrients. Too much insoluble fiber can irritate the gut lining. Soluble fiber, such as fruit fiber (pectin, psyllium, and oat bran) binds with water. It is also divided into two groups: fermentable and nonfermentable fiber. Fermentable fiber, such as beet pulp, is used by the gut bacteria to promote healthy gut flora.

Fat

Fat provides sustained energy to the body, and fat cells are the most efficient way that a dog's body stores energy for the future. Energy is measured in calories; and a gram of fat contains twice as many calories as a gram of either protein or carbohydrates. Fats are essential to build and maintain arteries and nerves, as well as for energy production on the cellular level, for kidney function, and to keep the dog's skin and fur coat shiny and supple. Some vitamins are only soluble (or digestible) in fat; these include vitamins A, D, E, and K.

Fat comes in two varieties: saturated and unsaturated. Saturated fat comes from animal sources. Unsaturated fat is generally derived from nuts, seeds, and fish oils.

Essential fatty acids are a significant component of fats. These are not manufactured in the dog's body and are therefore considered essential nutrients to eat. You have probably heard or read about omega-3 fatty acids. Omega-3 is rare in common foods; it must come from sources such as fish or flaxseeds. Olive oil is a great source of omega-9 fatty acids.

Cold-pressed oils are considered the best sources of essential fats, and why flaxseed oil is located in the refrigerated section at the health food store.

MICRONUTRIENTS

Foods that must be eaten in small quantities are called micronutrients. *Micro* means "small." Micronutrients are vitamins and minerals. Some minerals are referred to as trace minerals because the body needs only the minutest quantities of these to function. Micronutrients are absolutely essential to sound canine nutrition in numerous ways. Not only do vitamins and minerals promote a dog's health and physical development, they also regulate its metabolism and assist in the biochemical processes that release energy from digested food. Although a dog can synthesize some vitamins internally, it cannot synthesize any minerals whatsoever.

Vitamins

Today, many vitamins have been recognized, and it is likely that scientists will discover others. No vitamin acts alone. Together—and in conjunction with minerals—they perform in thousands of ways, impacting on digestion, metabolism, oxidation, reproduction, and growth. Fat-soluble vitamins include vitamins A, D, E, and K. These can be stored in the dog's liver and fatty tissues; in high doses, they can be toxic. Water-soluble vitamins include vitamin C and the various vitamin Bs (thiamin, riboflavin, niacin, B_6 [a.k.a. pyroxidine], folic acid, B_{12} [a.k.a. cyanocobalamin], pantothenic acid, pangamic acid, biotin, choline, and inositol). A dog must eat water-soluble vitamins every day because they are rapidly excreted in the urine and poop (a highly scientific term).

WHOLE-FOOD SOURCES OF VITAMINS

VITAMIN A	*Dairy:* Cheese, eggs, milk, and yogurt. *Fish:* Crab, haddock, halibut, herring, lobster, mackerel, oysters, salmon, swordfish, brook trout, and lake whitefish. *Meat:* Organ meats. *Grains:* Cornmeal. *Vegetables:* Asparagus, avocado, broccoli, carrots, green peas, leafy green vegetables, pumpkin, spinach, squash, sweet potato, and tomato. *Fruit:* Apples, apricots, bananas, blueberries, cherries, figs, grapes, mangos, nectarines, oranges, prunes, and tangerines.
VITAMIN B_6	*Vegetables*: Artichoke hearts and avocado. *Fruit*: Apples, apricots, bananas, dates, figs, mangos, plums, raisins, and strawberries.

WHOLE-FOOD SOURCES OF VITAMINS (CONT'D)

VITAMIN B$_{12}$	*Dairy:* Milk and yogurt. *Fish:* Tuna.
BIOTIN	*Dairy:* Eggs. *Fish:* Herring, oysters, and salmon. *Grains:* soy flour, oats, whole wheat, and nutritional yeast. *Vegetables:* Cauliflower and lima beans. *Meat:* Organ meat. *Nuts and Seeds:* Almonds, peanuts, and walnuts.
VITAMIN C	*Fruit:* Guava, orange, papayas, and strawberries. *Vegetables:* Alfalfa sprouts, asparagus, avocado, beets, bell pepper, broccoli, Brussels sprouts, cabbage, cauliflower, green beans, green peas, leafy green vegetables, lima beans, potato, soybeans, spinach, squash, sweet potato, and tomato.
CHOLINE	*Dairy:* Eggs. *Grains:* Wheat, soybeans, brown rice, and white rice.
VITAMIN D	Sunlight. *Dairy:* Swiss cheese, eggs, and milk. *Fish:* Cod liver oil, eel, herring, mackerel, salmon, sardines, and shrimp.

Whole-Food Sources of Vitamins (cont'd)

Vitamin E	*Dairy:* Eggs. *Grains:* Wheat germ. *Fruit:* Mangos. *Nuts and Seeds*: Almonds, hazelnuts, sunflower seeds. *Vegetables:* Avocado, kale, and sweet potato.
Folic Acid	*Dairy:* Eggs, milk, and yogurt. *Fruit:* Apricots, dates, and oranges. *Vegetables:* Artichoke hearts and avocado.
Inositol	Oats, egg yolk, herring, oysters, apples, blackberries, cherries, dates, grapefruit, kiwi, oranges, nectarines, peaches, prunes, wheat, beef liver, almonds, peanuts, walnuts, chicken liver, artichoke hearts, green beans, northern beans, lima beans, and navy beans.
Vitamin K	Soybean oil, beef liver, milk, yogurt, eggs, asparagus, broccoli, cabbage, cauliflower, green beans, peas, and chickpeas.
Niacin	Halibut, mackerel, salmon, shad, swordfish, tuna, whole wheat, dates, figs, guava, mangos, papayas, peaches, prunes, raisins, beef, lamb, pork, organ

WHOLE-FOOD SOURCES OF VITAMINS (CONT'D)

NIACIN (CONT'D)	meats, chicken, turkey, asparagus, avocado, mushrooms, green peas, potato, brown and white rice, soybeans, and squash.
PANTOTHENIC ACID	Apricots, bananas, dates, figs, guava, mangos, oranges, papayas, prunes, strawberries, milk, yogurt, chicken, turkey, and avocado.
RIBOFLAVIN	Apples, apricots, blueberries, boysenberries, dates, mangos, papayas, prunes, raisins, raspberries, strawberries, organ meats, milk, yogurt, alfalfa sprouts, asparagus, avocado, broccoli, Brussels sprouts, cauliflower, lima beans, mushrooms, green peas, rice, spinach, and squash.
THIAMINE	Bananas, blueberries, dates, figs, grapes, guava, mangos, oranges, papayas, prunes, raisins, milk, yogurt, asparagus, avocado, broccoli, cauliflower, green beans, leeks, lima beans, green peas, potato, rice, soybeans, spinach, and sweet potato.

There is an easy practice to guarantee that your dog gets all the vitamins and minerals it requires. Include a rainbow of colored fruits and vegetables in your dog's meals throughout the course of a week: green, yellow, orange, red, purple, and blue. A dog's meals do not have to include the whole spectrum in a single serving or even in a single day to benefit them.

Minerals

Minerals regulate diverse physiological and biochemical processes, including those pertaining to body fluids, nerve conduction, muscle contractions, and the structural integrity of the cell walls and membranes. Dogs cannot make use of any other foods or vitamins unless their diet also includes minerals, which are involved in many biochemical processes. When people refer to trace minerals, they are talking about those minerals the

WHOLE-FOOD SOURCES OF MINERALS	
CALCIUM	Bulgur wheat, cheese, cottage cheese, clams, mussels, oysters, salmon, carob flour, cornmeal, soy flour, figs, papayas, milk, yogurt, almonds, brazil nuts, broccoli, and leafy green vegetables.
CHROMIUM	Cheese, apples, clams, plums, prunes, chicken breast and skin, peanuts, thyme, and black pepper.

Whole-Food Sources of Minerals (cont'd)

Copper	Zucchini, pumpkin, chicken, turkey, pears, dates, figs, and apricots.
Iodine	Cheese, eggs, cod liver oil, cod, haddock, oysters, yogurt, kelp (seaweed), and table salt.
Iron	Oats, bulgar wheat, eggs, abalone, saltwater bass, striped mullet, saltwater mussels, oysters, sardines, scallops, weakfish, cornmeal, rye, whole wheat, dates, figs, raisins, beef, lamb, beef and lamb liver, beef and lamb kidneys, chicken, turkey, chicken liver, avocado, Brussels sprouts, leafy green vegetables, butter beans, lima beans, kidney beans, lentils, green peas, pumpkin seeds, sesame seeds, white rice, soybeans, acorn squash, butternut squash, and Hubbard squash.
Magnesium	Oats, cod, haddock, mackerel, striped mullet, oysters, shrimp, sole, cornmeal, rye, whole wheat, dates, figs, papayas, prunes, raisins, tamarinds, milk, yogurt, peanuts, sesame seeds, chicken, turkey, avocado, beets, leafy green vegetables,

Whole-Food Sources of Minerals (cont'd)

Magnesium (cont'd)	carrots, cauliflower, leeks, chickpeas, green peas, potato, pumpkin, brown rice, and spinach.
Manganese	Oats, blackberries, blueberries, boysenberries, dates, figs, grapes, pineapple, raisins, raspberries, strawberries, peanuts, and avocado.
Molybdenum	Barley, buckwheat, beef kidney, lamb, lean pork, green beans, lentils, strawberries, yams, and tomato.
Phosphorus	Barley, bulgar wheat, oats, cheese, cottage cheese, eggs, abalone, freshwater bass, bluefish, carp, clams, cod, crabs, freshwater crayfish, cusk, eel, sole, haddock, halibut, herring, ocean perch, oysters, red snapper, salmon, scallops, shrimp, smelt, swordfish, brook trout, tuna, cornmeal, rye, whole wheat, raisins, beef, lamb, organ meats, milk, yogurt, brazil nuts, cashews, peanuts, pumpkin seeds, sesame seeds, chicken, turkey, mushrooms, green peas, brown rice, butternut squash, and sweet potato.

Whole-Food Sources of Minerals (cont'd)

Potassium	Cottage cheese, saltwater bass, bonito, carp, clams, cod, haddock, halibut, Pacific and lake herring, striped mullet, mussels, oysters, red snapper, salmon, sole, weakfish, buckwheat flour, cornmeal, soy flour, apples, apricots, bananas, dates, figs, guava, papayas, plums, prunes, raisins, tangelos, beef, lamb, organ meats, milk, yogurt, almonds, brazil nuts, cashews, peanuts, sesame seeds, chicken, turkey, artichoke, asparagus, avocado, beets, broccoli, cauliflower, leafy green vegetables, lima beans, mushrooms, green peas, bell pepper, potato, pumpkin, spinach, squash, sweet potato, and tomato.
Selenium	Tuna, bananas, barley, noodles, brown and white rice, beef, chicken, lamb liver, beef liver and kidneys, pork kidneys, cashew nuts, garlic, mushrooms, navy beans, and molasses.
Zinc	Cheese, cottage cheese, eggs, rye flour, dates, guava, papayas, raisins, most fruits have small amounts, milk, yogurt, peanuts, sesame seeds, chicken, and turkey.

body requires in the minutest proportions. Trace minerals are essential elements of a good diet.

Minerals include calcium, chloride, chromium, copper, iodine, iron, magnesium, manganese, molybdenum, phosphorus, potassium, selenium, sulfur, and zinc. The list truly goes on and on. The best sources of minerals are vegetables, fruits, and legumes, although minerals are also found in other foods.

WATER

Water is as crucial for optimal health as any food. Change the water in your dog's bowl every day; your dog needs plenty of fresh water to drink. If you can provide spring water, that is ideal, for fresh water contains trace minerals. Filtered water is also good, although it contains no trace minerals; when you filter water to eliminate toxins, you also eliminate essential nutrients. Never use distilled water because it has been demineralized.

Watch out for a few water hazards. The first one is chlorine. Chlorine is nearly unavoidable these days in tap water, since it is added to the drinking supply at treatment plants in order to kill the microbes—bacteria, viruses, and parasites—that cause diseases. Chlorine is toxic especially to the kidneys, liver, and heart, and it depletes the body of vitamin E and other essential nutrients. It is a strong oxidizing agent.

The second water hazard is lead. Lead comes from old pipes, so you must run the cold water for a couple of minutes to give the standing water in the pipes a chance to clear out. Then it should be drinkable. Never use hot tap water for drinking, as that strips lead from pipes. A third potential hazard is the nitrates in water that run off fertilized farmland and into the drinking supply in rural agricultural areas.

You must also keep in mind—when you are out walking with your dogs—that water in the streams, creeks, and swamps you pass can cause them stomach ailments if they drink from these supplies. Open water may be stagnant and contain microbes, and/or be polluted by chemicals. In my community in Maryland, the sewer system has a history of leaking into the surrounding waters because the pipes are old and rusty and have sprung holes. If your area has flooding or excessive rain, this may cause an overflow of your sewers as well. Do your best to be vigilant about water.

HIDDEN DEFICITS

Now that we have considered the nutrients your dog needs and their whole-food sources, let us look at some of the hidden ways good nutrition may be sabotaged. Ideally, your dog should receive all the nutrients he or she needs from the meals you provide; however, there are several potential deficits that can rob your dog's food of its nutritional values. These may affect your beloved companion animal and its health even if you home-cook and use whole-food ingredients.

Refinement

During food processing, nutrients in foods are taxed out. While you can replace vitamins and minerals synthetically, as processed dog food does with artificial ingredients, the choice is less than ideal. An example of a refined food that you may find yourself cooking with is white flour versus whole wheat flour. Whole wheat contains more fiber, vitamin K, phosphorus, and magnesium than enriched white flour. Try to use whole, fresh ingredients whenever possible.

Overfarming

Did you know that even the fresh produce we buy these days is often deficient in vitamins and minerals? Farmers sometimes overwork their land until the soil in which plants are grown is spent. Without enough nutrients to draw in through their roots, plants have diminished food values. That is why gardeners use fertilizer and compost to enhance the soil. As a consumer, it is virtually impossible to determine which produce comes from overworked, chemically supplemented, and nutrient-deficient soil unless the food product says "organically certified."

Soil Leaching

In addition to overfarming, spent soil is often the result of environmental effects like natural leaching by excessive rainfall. Excess rain can wash and lift minerals out of the soil, so they lay on the surface where the roots of plants are deprived of them. What you end up with, again, are plants lacking in essential nutrients.

Pesticides

Pesticides are poisons designed to kill bugs and parasites that feed on plants, in order to make the plants grow well. Pesticides are also sprayed on the outside of produce to repel insects during transport and while they are stocked on the shelves in some supermarkets. There are some 300 pesticides used on crops sold in the United States. Over time, the pesticide absorbed into your dog's tissues becomes toxic. The systems of the body that filter out harmful elements and eliminate waste become polluted and ultimately fail to do their jobs. The result is discomfort and disease.

SUPPLEMENTS

Perfection in dog food is hard to achieve, as you can see. That is why, above and beyond feeding a dog balanced meals made with whole ingredients, regularly supplementing those meals with vitamins, minerals, and fatty acids is the best way to ensure the dog's needs are being entirely met. I recommend a weekly schedule of four supplements: Healthy Powder, wheat germ oil, flaxseed oil, and love. Love alone is not enough!

You need to gradually add supplements to your dog's diet in order to give the body time to adjust (see Chapter 5). If your dog has not yet completed the transition to a fresh homemade diet from processed dog food, wait until you have completed the switch to begin supplementing its food. See Chapter 5 for appropriate transitional feeding instructions.

How much of a supplement is too much? The recommendations that follow are reasonably conservative. When in doubt, however, give less. Much depends on the size of your pooch. Remember always to practice common sense when you are planning your dog's menu. For obvious reasons, supplements should never be used to substitute for a wholesome balanced diet. Talk to your holistic vet for an expert opinion.

Believe it or not, oversupplementing can be just as bad, or worse, than undersupplementing because certain nutrients, such as fat-soluble vitamins, can and do become toxic in excess. Whereas water-soluble vitamins get flushed out of the body through the urine stream, fat can be stored in the liver and tissues, and fat-soluble vitamins get stored along with it.

Here are some general guidelines, although they are not set in stone.

Weekly Feeding Schedule for Supplements

Monday	Tuesday	Wednesday	Thursday	Friday	Saturday	Sunday
Healthy Powder	Healthy Powder	Healthy Powder	Healthy Powder			
Wheat germ oil	Wheat germ oil	Wheat germ oil	Wheat germ oil			
Flaxseed oil	Flaxseed oil	Flaxseed oil	Flaxseed oil	Flaxseed oil	Flaxseed oil	
Love	Love	Love	Love	Love	Love	Love

Unless otherwise directed by your veterinarian, you may supplement your dog's diet four days a week with Healthy Powder and wheat germ oil (vitamin E), and six days a week with flaxseed oil (essential fatty acids). Supplement with love seven days a week!

Please double-check my feeding instructions with your trusted holistic veterinarian.

Healthy Powder

Once a day, four days a week, give small dogs (up to 35 pounds) 2 teaspoons, medium dogs (35–60 pounds) 3 teaspoons, large and giant dogs (above 60 pounds) 2 tablespoons.

The recipe for Healthy Powder follows; see page 74.

Wheat Germ Oil

Once a day, five days a week, give small dogs ½ tablespoon, medium dogs 1 tablespoon, large dogs 1½ tablespoons, and giant breeds 2 tablespoons.

Please refrigerate any oils. Vitamin E helps make a dog's skin and coat healthy and supple. It is a valuable antioxidant.

Flaxseed Oil

Once a day, give small dogs ½ tablespoon, medium dogs 1 tablespoon, large dogs 1½ tablespoons, and giant dogs 2 tablespoons.

You can locate flaxseed oil in the refrigerated section of a health food store. The omega-3 fatty acids found in the oil are essential to a dog's healthy coat.

Love

Give dogs of all sizes abundant amounts of love whenever and however you can. Love them with your voice, your touch, by playing with them, and through responsible care. Love is never toxic and dogs will always return it unconditionally. Science has proven love is as good for you as for your beloved companion animal.

Healthy Powder

Healthy Powder is economical to make and the recipe is incredibly simple. In a pinch, you can get a supply of this supplement from a holistic veterinarian, but if you can make a whole batch to keep at home in your refrigerator, you should not run out frequently. Here is what goes into it and why:

- Nutritional yeast (*not* brewer's yeast, which is a beverage industry by-product), which is the base of the powder, is a great source of phosphorus and other nutrients, especially the B-complex vitamins. You can find nutritional yeast in powder or flakes in health food stores and quality supermarkets. Caution: Dogs may become allergic to the proteins in yeast.

- Lecithin contains the B vitamins, choline, and inositol, as well as iron and linoleic acid, one of the essential fatty acids. You can find lecithin granules in health food stores.

- Kelp or chelated seaweed powder contains iodine, iron, magnesium, phosphorus, sodium, and other trace minerals that your pet requires. Since seaweed (which floats around in the ocean) does not have a root system, it can absorb minerals throughout its membranes and does not lose any. Kelp or chelated seaweed powder is also available at the health food store.

- Eggshell powder (recipe to follow) provides the calcium necessary to accompany the phosphorus found in the nutritional yeast and kelp. These two minerals must always go hand in hand in a balanced diet. The only other potential source of calcium for this recipe is bone meal powder. Consumer advocate Ralph Nader conducted a study on bone meal that was alarming, however. When his research group tested a wide sampling of brands sold in health food stores, they discovered that most contained lead. Lead is toxic, so why take the risk?

- Vitamin C powder is optional, although vitamin C is an essential nutrient. You can make it by grinding up a tablet from the health food store or pharmacy.

Warning

Never—ever—supplement the diets of pregnant and lactating bitches or puppies unless you are following the specific advice of a veterinarian. It may seem counterintuitive, since they clearly need more calories in their diets to promote the growth of the puppy (or puppies), yet their internal chemistry easily can be thrown out of whack. Give these dogs more food—if they want it—and spare the supplements.

Healthy Powder

2 cups nutritional yeast (flakes or powder)
1 cup lecithin granules
¼ cup kelp or chelated seaweed powder
5 teaspoons eggshell powder (see page 75)
1,000 milligrams vitamin C powder (optional)

Mix all of the ingredients thoroughly. Store refrigerated in an airtight container.

YEAST SUBSTITUTE: Sometimes dogs are allergic to yeast. If your dog is one of these, eliminate nutritional yeast from the recipe and add a tablespoon of flaxseed oil when you serve the Healthy Powder. An allergy to yeast is common and can be provoked if you are not cautious. Your vet can help you determine if this is an issue.

One of my neighbors had been feeding her dog a tablespoon of nutritional yeast every day for months as a natural means to repel fleas. By the time we spoke about the problem, her dog had developed chronic ear infections and its ears were giving off a funny odor. My neighbor and her pet had been to the vet, where antibiotics and eardrops were prescribed. Once the condition cleared up, they stopped treatment and the condition returned, every time. (They did this more than once.) What this woman had not considered was how much yeast already existed in her dog's diet. In addition to the nutritional yeast she was feeding it daily, her dog was eating a commercial pet food that contained yeast. Her dog's immune system had gone into overload.

Based on my recommendation, this neighbor eliminated yeast from her dog's diet altogether. She began home-cooking for her dog, following the transition diet in Chapter 5, and started supplementing her pet's meals with a small amount of flaxseed oil. Within a month her dog's problem was completely cleared up, and today she feeds it the healthy powder without the yeast.

KELP SUBSTITUTE: If you have difficulty locating kelp or chelated seaweed powder, substitute ¾ teaspoon of iodized salt and ¼ cup of alfalfa powder. Or, you may want to skip the iodized salt and substitute alfalfa powder alone, if your dog has high blood pressure or a heart condition.

See the Resources section at the back of this book for mail-order sources of kelp powder.

Barker's Grub

Eggshell Powder

Eggshell powder is the absolute best source of calcium around. Making it is also a great way not to waste raw materials. If you eat eggs or cook with eggs, toss the empty shells in a clean plastic container until you are ready to make another big batch.

Sterilize 12 or more shells by baking them in the oven for 15 to 20 minutes at 350 degrees. Grind them finely—try one of those small electric coffee-bean grinders or use a mortar and pestle—and save the eggshell powder in your refrigerator. If the powder is kept cool and dry, it should maintain for quite a long time. (Throw it out if it changes color and looks moldy.) Eggshell powder is an essential ingredient in the Healthy Powder recipe. If you don't want to use eggshells, you can use bone meal instead.

ADDING SUPPLEMENTS TO THE DIET

If your dog has never received supplements, you will need to transition them slowly into its diet. You can start with eggshell powder and flaxseed oil for one month. In the first week, begin supplementing by one-fourth of the recommended dosage for each day. Each week increase the dosage by another one-fourth. Be attentive to whether your dog is experiencing diarrhea or has other symptoms; the supplement may not agree with your dog.

In the second month, if all goes as planned, you can add in the remaining supplements, moving to a full dose of Healthy Powder and wheat germ oil, too.

Daily Calcium Supplement

Yield: 1 tablespoon

If you have a single eggshell left over from breakfast, use it to make a daily calcium supplement that is appropriate for dogs transitioning to supplements, as well as those with yeast allergies.

1 eggshell, finely ground
1 tablespoon flaxseed oil
1 teaspoon kelp or chelated seaweed powder

Boil an eggshell for 5 minutes, and then grind it to a powder. You can do this in a small coffee grinder or by hand. The shell should be as finely ground as possible. You can also purchase ground eggshells from a health food store, but homemade powder is better.

Add the flaxseed oil and kelp or chelated seaweed powder, and combine thoroughly in a small mixing bowl.

To serve, add a small pinch of the mixture to your dog's fresh food.

A WORD ABOUT ENZYME SUPPLEMENTS

Enzymes are responsible for the myriad chemical processes of digestion. There are several types, each specific to a different protein, carbohydrate, fat, or vegetable. Needless to say, we still do not know as much as we would like about them. However, you cannot go wrong by supplementing a dog's diet with enzymes.

Dr. Michael W. Fox recommends adding a tablespoon of "live" food such as chopped alfalfa sprouts, mung bean sprouts, or lentil sprouts once or twice a week to your dog's meal. This practice will provide an excellent source of enzymes and nutrients. Alternatively you can add freeze-dried super-blue green algae or spirulina. There are also a couple of beneficial enzyme supplements called Prozyme and Florazyme, which you can get from holistic veterinarians.

Cooked food needs to be accompanied by a digestive enzyme supplement. Otherwise the pancreas becomes overworked. Because it has yeast, the Healthy Powder has live enzymes in it. If your dog has allergies to yeast, Prozyme can be substituted.

Chapter 4

Special Cases

The Healing Power of Home Cooking

Nutrition plays an active role in overall health, both preventive and restorative, as well as in behavior. There are also some commonplace developmental stages and life circumstances that require specialized nutrition. Follow the Rotation Diet described in Chapter 5, with the dietary modifications indicated below that address these special cases.

PREGNANT AND LACTATING FEMALES

When your female dog is pregnant or nursing puppies, it should eat a diet that is modified only by quantity. "Making puppies" requires a greater number of calories. Instead of feeding the dog twice or three times a day, feed it as frequently as four times a day and give the dog as much food as it wants. The distribution of ingredients is still going to be 50 percent protein, 25 percent carbohydrates, and 25 percent vegetables.

You may supplement the diets of pregnant and nursing females, although it is critical not to oversupplement with calcium. I cannot emphasize this too much. Please check with your veterinarian when you find your dog is pregnant to determine the right level of calcium supplementation for your dog's body weight. Dogs are pregnant for only nine weeks, and they typically nurse until the puppies' teeth come in.

Even though pregnant and nursing females should continue to follow the Rotation Diet, it is unadvisable to put them on the Purification Meal at the end of the month (see Chapter 5).

PUPPIES

Puppies will continue to nurse their mother's milk until they are five or six weeks old. The mother dog will wean them naturally around that time. Generally, human beings should not intervene in this process, which could go on longer than this. By forcing the weaning too soon you can instill separation anxiety in a puppy that it may carry throughout its life. There's no need for it, since ravenous puppies ultimately long for solid food in their bellies. The strongest benefit of nursing to pups is how it helps build their immune systems.

The mother dog will wean her puppies off milk somewhat gradually. You may also find your puppies expressing an interest in the content of their mother's food bowl while they are still nursing, perhaps as soon as five weeks of age. At that point, put out some mushy food especially for the puppies.

Up until the age of two, puppies require a growth diet that includes extra protein and a greater number of calories than the diet of an adult dog. This contributes to the development of healthy tissue, bones, and organs, even the brain. You should feed a puppy three times each day, and each feeding should include a mix of 60 percent protein and 20 percent each of carbohydrates and vegetables. (See the Puppy Food section in Chapter 6.)

As soon as a puppy begins eating solid food exclusively you can begin supplementing its diet (see Chapter 3). Use the quantity of supplements recommended for its body weight, and adjust the amount as it grows heavier.

OLDER DOGS

As they age, sometimes dogs slow down. This is perfectly normal. Therefore, as with other adult dogs, you would feed them the Rotation Diet (see Chapter 5) in a ratio of calories derived from 50 percent protein, 25 percent carbohydrates, and 25 percent vegetables. However, to accommodate a decreased metabolism, you would give them slightly smaller portions.

You can tell whether or not your dog's reduced appetite is from illness and not general aging if he or she exhibits the usual symptoms of an unhealthy animal, such as lethargy, a dull coat, and runny eyes. When in doubt, check with your veterinarian.

ADOPTED SHELTER OR RESCUE ANIMALS

There are some essential principles of nutrition it is wise to consider when you adopt an animal from a shelter or take an animal otherwise in need of rescue into your home. First, remember that your new dog is an individual, one with whom you are not yet familiar. You will need to take time and pay close attention to learn its needs.

For ten days, you should feed your new dog friend a diet that is bland—a simple chicken and rice, or simple beef and rice dish (the Transition Diet; see Chapter 5). Do not give it any supplements. After ten days, you begin adding the flaxseed oil supplement at half the dosage recommended in Chapter 3. After a week, go to the full dosage. The dog's system may not be used to adequate nutrition, so you need to make the dietary shift gradually.

The first couple of days after bringing your dog home from the shelter, be especially sure to neither underfeed nor overfeed it, to give its digestive system time to adjust. As a rule of thumb, up to two cups of food at a feeding is not too much or too little for most dogs. If the dog still acts hungry—and because the dog may be malnourished—rather than increasing the amount of food above two cups, feed it more frequently—at least three times a day—unless it is an extremely large animal.

After ten days, you can slowly add vegetables to the meat and rice (about one-half cup at a time), and you can moderate the dog's intake according to whether it is now putting on weight. Then you begin to go by the general feeding instructions for healthy puppies or adult dogs (see pages 80 and 119). Consult your holistic veterinarian during the process. In particular you want to ensure that they receive adequate protein.

A dog that has been malnourished may exhibit a wide variety of behavioral symptoms, from lethargy to agitation. They may overeat or undereat. Once I found a Bluetick Coonhound by the edge of the water in the Black Water Refuge, a wildlife area of upland woods in Maryland. Hunters sometimes abandon such a dog because it is not a good hunter, they bred too many dogs at one time, or the dog has gotten old. A man in a nearby trailer home told me that this dog had been living for weeks on cat food and cat excrement. Later I named her Quinn.

I could lift Quinn with one arm, she was so malnourished—skin and bones. She also had no hair on the outside of her ears. Her previous owners must have kept her penned up and hungry so she would have more motivation to hunt. She had lost all her short front teeth because she had been chewing on cage wire, and she required a root canal for one of the canines.

My vet thought the tooth had been smashed with a blunt object.

Quinn was head-shy (shrank away from being touched) as I placed her in my car and we drove home. That night she would not even lie down, she was so insecure; she stood swaying like a drunkard, even though she was weak and emaciated. I tried to make a little bed for her and convince her to lie down, but she watched me incessantly and suspiciously from a distance. She also could not eat because she would not take her eyes off of me. Finally I went to bed. She put her head on the mattress where she stood, closed her eyes, and finally let me pet her. Soon I took her in the bed (although she reeked) and she went to sleep.

The next morning Quinn gulped down a bowlful of chicken and white rice. I fed her three times that day, and for the next ten days she either ate this meal or beef and rice. Then I added vegetables and eggs to her diet and her coat became thicker and shinier. She grew hair back on her ears, and once again she was a regal huntress.

I found Quinn in the fall when I had to put sweaters on her because she was shivering so badly from cold. She lacked body fat. The veterinarian estimated that she was three or four years old, but she looked much older because she had whelped puppies many times. No dog should be bred more than once a year. After a month and a half she started looking and feeling better; her energy was high. Originally she was thirty-five to forty pounds in size, which for her breed is nothing! Today she weighs about seventy-nine pounds, and she is not considered fat. No one at the dog park could recognize her after six months; she became young and vital, and absolutely was not the same dog. Quinn lived with me for six months until I found a good loving home for her.

Post-Surgery, Post-Trauma, and Stress

If your dog has been spayed, neutered, or undergone another surgical procedure; is recovering from a car crash or other trauma; or has been experiencing general life stress, you may want to feed it food that is gentle on the stomach, such as chicken and rice. Give the dog plenty of cooked leafy green vegetables and roots, such as turnips and carrots. You can also mix a little kelp powder into its food. All of these are high in the vitamins and minerals it will need for healing what ails it. Make sure it gets its flaxseed oil supplement every day. Remember to be extra kind and loving.

Allergies and Skin Disorders

Common signs that a dog is having an allergic reaction to something it ate or otherwise contacted are constant scratching, dry flaky patches of skin, red and swollen eyes, and tiny bumps on its body. (These may also be indicative of a dry environment.) Other skin and coat problems include dandruff and a sort of general dullness that make the dog look dirty and unwell. Some dogs develop chronic, even bloody diarrhea in response to one or more allergens in their food.

When a dog is allergic to a food ingredient, its symptoms should disappear after the ingredient is eliminated from the diet. A dog may also become hypersensitive to normally benign substances when overexposed to them. There are food-allergen skin tests that your holistic veterinarian can administer. It is likely that your dog will be placed on a bland diet for several weeks and you will be encouraged after a while to reintroduce other foods one at a time. If the symptoms recur, you have found your culprit. This course takes patience and diligence.

FLEAS AND TICKS

Infestations such as fleas can have severe consequences. Dogs deficient in vitamin B are said to be more attractive to these little buggers. To compensate, add nutritional yeast and garlic to the dog's food. You can also add a tiny amount of apple cider vinegar or red wine vinegar—less than a teaspoon per day—just before serving. (More than that and the dog probably would not eat the meal.) Do this once a day during spring or summer to repel insects. The vinegar balances the amount of acid and alkaline in the body.

GASTROINTESTINAL PROBLEMS

If your dog is prone to gas, or has a deep chest, it may develop bloat and torsion. But beware; I have seen a miniature dog with these problems, so it is not just the giants that get them. These are two conditions that, in combination, can be fatal. Bloat is gas and torsion is a twisting in the intestines that prevents the gas from escaping. If your dog is "windy" feed it small meals spaced throughout the day. And be sure to moderate the number of vegetables it is getting; keep it to one veggie per meal. Also avoid vigorous exercise after meals. Another solution is to give the dog some activated charcoal, which is available at any health food store. This helps eliminate gas and absorb toxins. Check with your holistic vet for an appropriate dosage for your dog's size and weight.

In addition, for gastrointestinal problems as diverse as colitis, stomach ulcers, and bacterial infections, you may give your dog some unpasteurized "live" culture yogurt. Yogurt coats the stomach and reintroduces natural flora, which aid in digestion, to the intestines. Yogurt is acceptable for all gastrointestinal conditions, even if a dog is allergic to yeast.

A small dog can eat two tablespoons of yogurt, a medium dog can eat four tablespoons, and a large dog can tolerate six to eight tablespoons. Because yogurt contains high levels of amino acids, your dog may find it slightly sedative to the nervous system as well (like when you go to sleep after eating a turkey dinner).

DIABETES

The pancreas is a tiny organ that secretes insulin into the blood-stream to control blood sugar levels. It can produce too much or, in the case of diabetes, too little. Dogs with diabetes must eat fewer calories, and low-fat and high-fiber meals, and must have no refined sugars whatsoever. (I do not recommend sugar for dogs, anyhow.) They will also need to be given insulin injections to manage their blood sugar levels, so you will have to work closely with your veterinarian. Many vets will recommend that insulin injections be coordinated with the feeding schedule.

Also important, you must learn to keep your dog's diet incredibly steady so its insulin levels will be exactly maintained. This means feeding your dog the same thing, the same amount, and at the same time every day. Talk to your vet about it.

KIDNEY PROBLEMS

Make sure your dog is getting enough vitamin C in its diet to acidify its urine. However, if your dog has kidney disease of any kind, do not give it supplements except for flaxseed oil. Because one of the jobs of the kidneys is to purify the body, when you supplement they begin working harder.

The parts of the kidneys that filter blood are called *glomeruli* (found in the outer cortex), and these may cease functioning for many reasons. A new scientific study conducted at Morris Animal Clinic has been gaining a lot of attention among veterinarians. It reports that flaxseed oil can actually reverse kidney damage. Within as few as three days, they have seen near-miraculous remissions. Flaxseed oil is simply an amazing natural source of essential fatty acids. Another good source of these is safflower oil.

GUM DISEASE

Yes, dogs get dental disease. This is why you should give your dog raw meat and bones to gnaw on from time to time. The chewiness of the intact meat works like a suction device to remove plaque. A dog that has lost its teeth will have trouble eating and maintaining weight, and will feel pain. Furthermore, there is a secondary tier of problems caused by dental diseases. If the bacteria in your dog's mouth get out of hand, gum disease can lead to infections of the kidneys, heart, and other organs, the germs having been transported in the bloodstream. So a clean mouth is pretty darn important.

POISONING

While I am on the subject of special cases, I should say a few words about poisoning. Our dogs today are not wild creatures, although they still possess the inherent hunting and foraging instincts of wild creatures, and there are many substances in our homes that are toxic to them, which they might eat or drink. What are the signs of poisoning? If your dog is continuously vomiting, it is a good idea to contact your veterinarian immediately or call your Poison Control Center. Not all poisons make a dog vomit, however. If your dog is having a seizure or seems unusually lethargic, these may also be signs of poisoning. Again, seek immediate help.

ARTHRITIS

Arthritis affects many dogs. It can be a congenital condition, a product of trauma, or a function of old age. Sometimes you see young dogs with arthritis. In any case, it causes stiffness and swelling in the joints and a loss of cartilage. There are two natural means that I have seen to be helpful in coping with the symptoms of arthritic inflammation. The first is cartilage supplements. There are many sources of cartilage available from health food stores. Talk to your holistic veterinarian about which may be right for your dog. The second is yucca root, which can go right into the meals. Yucca root looks like a cross between a sweet potato and a turnip, when it is peeled. You can recognize it as a long, oblong root with what resembles tree bark on the outside.

BEHAVIORAL PROBLEMS

Proper nutrition is essential for your dog's psychological, as well as physical, well-being. The behavior and emotions of dogs are as complex as those of humans; and when people speak to me about their dogs, at least three out of five go on to describe some sort of strange or unwanted activities: aggression, excessive barking, lethargy, or garbage-eating. Nutritional deficiencies can cause depression, poor vision, and poor mental focus, and can adversely affect learning ability. A number of physical, emotional, and mental conditions can manifest themselves in odd behavior as a result of an improper diet. Vitamin and mineral deficiencies in particular may lead to hunger cravings that the dog is seeking to alleviate. When troubleshooting a behavioral problem, generally you must respond with a combination of approaches. Correcting nutritional imbalances is always the first of these.

Dogs often develop behavioral problems owing to deprivation of basic nutritional needs (fat, for example). A commercial pet food label might read "Reduced Fat" to attract customers to purchase the product for their overweight dogs. In actuality, all one need do to counteract obesity is reduce the carbohydrates, not the fat. Fat is an essential nutrient and should not make a dog more overweight. A deficiency of fat can cause depression and aggression.

Depression and Lethargy

Depression can be caused by a lack of fatty acids, and a dull coat is a clear sign that dogs are lacking enough nutrient fatty acids. Its symptoms are withdrawal and lethargy, and an unwillingness to learn or interact. Ninety-nine percent of the shelter dogs I have observed are depressed from malnutrition, combined with a lack of love and affection. Once the dog begins to receive proper nutrition, you should see its depression clear up dramatically within a month. Consult your veterinarian if lethargy persists.

Aggression

Some breeds, like Rottweilers, are prone to becoming more aggressive than others. (By the way, I happen to know several very sweet and gentle-natured Rottweilers.) In general, these dogs need a higher level of fat and carbohydrates in their diets to keep them calm. If your dog is aggressive toward other dogs or human beings, try giving it less protein. But remember, the causes of aggression can be varied and might not have to do with diet alone. Feed it the Aggression Reduction Meal in Chapter 6 to strike a new balance.

If your dog is still on a processed food diet when you decide to attempt to cure this behavior with home cooking, first feed it the Transitional Diet described in Chapter 5, then continue with the Aggression Reduction Meal. Be sure to go slowly. The dog's behavior should gradually transform over a month or so. With the conjunction of herbal remedies that a holistic veterinarian recommends, aggression should be fairly easily dissipated.

Home Wrecking

This problem most frequently occurs after adopting a new puppy or dog. Moving to a new home can be enormously stressful for a pet. To make your dog feel more comfortable and less anxious, feed it all natural foods and make sure it is receiving appropriate supplementation. Adding fat to a dog's diet will have a sedative effect, as will using certain herbs. Some Bach flower remedies specifically relieve panic attacks and calm the nerves. The drops my vet recommended for one of the dogs I fostered was called Rescue Remedy. You can find Bach flower remedies at the health food store.

Feces Eating

Health professionals call this "pica" and describe the behavior as "depraved appetite." One theory about what causes feces eating is that essential vitamins are lacking in the dog's meals, so the dog is trying to find them wherever it can. This behavior may also be an obsessive-compulsive disorder caused by brain chemistry or emotional trauma. It may also indicate that a dog is not properly digesting its food.

Dogs that are boarded in kennels or in shelters, or even those that are crated at home, sometimes develop this behavior; possibly it is linked to boredom. Other dogs develop this odd behavior because they were punished as puppies for making poop messes. To clean up the feces and prevent future trauma, it eats them.

Some animal species, such as rats and rabbits, naturally eat their own feces for nutrition. Scientists call this "refection." It has been found that bacteria in the intestines produce some vitamins not present in the original food the animals ate, such as B vitamins. In such instances, the animal's craving for feces may indicate a deficiency.

You can try to break the pattern of feces eating through a combination of training and high-vitamin foods, such as raw chopped liver. Liver has a plethora of essential nutrients, such as vitamin A and many B vitamins. If you are concerned about meat-borne illness, cook the meat to 180 degrees Fahrenheit. Some nutrients will be diminished, although it will retain most of its nutritional value. Another way to prepare the chopped liver is to pan-sear it so that the outside is sterilized. You can also give your dog special enzyme powders called Prozyme and Florazyme, which contain digestive enzymes and minerals; these are available through holistic veterinarians or some pet supply stores.

Dirt Eating

Soil is eaten by many species, including human beings, for its trace mineral content. People in certain parts of rural America have been known to eat clay and many pregnant women have reported the craving to eat dirt. Free-ranging dogs in India often eat dirt. This behavior is particularly telling if a dog is eating processed food; it may mean that some of the trace minerals it requires for good health are missing. Dogs can exhibit this behavior in different seasons, depending on their changing needs.

Garbage Eating

Like feces eating and dirt eating, garbage eating is likely to be a mistaken attempt to satisfy a natural urge for trace minerals and vitamins. A dog may also eat garbage if it is underfed or always hungry. If a dog is not getting the nutrients it requires, it will scrounge for food. Wild dogs are natural scavengers, and that instinct comes into play whenever a domesticated dog craves sustenance. Consult a holistic veterinarian to see what can be done to improve your dog's nutritional status.

Begging

This behavior is connected to the dog's instinct for food sharing. Some people do not mind feeding their dogs at the table; others think it is a violation of the world order. The way to get around nuisance begging can be simple: when you are about to eat a meal, also give some food to your dog. A dog will get into the routine of eating its share and leaving you alone. Food sharing helps dogs feel involved, not separated, from their family, and it is emotionally satisfying. When dogs do not feel deprived, food becomes less attractive.

Chapter 5

Cooking for Your Dog

Preparing the Kitchen and Transitioning to Home Cooking

At Barker's Grub, cooking for dogs is my business, but I also find it extremely pleasurable. While I mix my customers' weekly orders, I put on some loud classical music and dance around the kitchen. I occasionally indulge myself in the late afternoon by sipping on a small glass of port wine or dry sherry. Most of all, I enjoy the satisfaction of knowing that the dogs I feed are getting the most wholesome and healthy food that is available. Once you get the hang of it, I think you'll feel the same way.

KITCHEN EQUIPMENT

You need very little specific equipment to cook the Barker's Grub meals. Since we are cooking fresh whole foods, most of the prep work lies in chopping vegetables and meats into bite-sized pieces of about a quarter inch. In addition to chopping knives, you will need utensils, mixing bowls, and cooking pots. You'll also need enough containers to hold the food you've made in your freezer throughout the week. Here's a more complete list:

- 2 sharp chopping knives, one for meat and one for vegetables
- A chopping board (I use a lightweight plastic one that can go right into the dishwasher)

- A colander, to drain your fruits and vegetables
- A food processor, with a large capacity, for chopping and/or pureeing meats and vegetables
- A small electric coffee grinder, for powdering herbs and supplements
- 2 super-large pots that will each hold up to 2 gallons of liquid. I prefer cast-iron so that they won't slip or spill from the stovetop (for the weekly recipes)
- 2 pots that will hold 8 cups of liquid (for the single-serving recipes)
- 1 slotted spoon
- 1 pasta ladle
- 1 spaghetti spoon
- 1 ice cream scoop
- 1 skillet, 12 inches in diameter and with a 2-inch rim
- 2 large mixing bowls that will each hold up to 2½ gallons of liquid (for the weekly recipe variations; I prefer metal because it is lighter and easier to clean)
- 2 small mixing bowls that will each hold up to 1 gallon of liquid (for the single-serving recipes)
- 2 or 3 wooden spoons
- A rolling pin
- Cookie cutters, any style
- 2 12- by 18-inch cookie sheets
- A good-sized freezer, to hold your dog's meals for the week ahead
- Numerous small plastic food containers or reusable zippered bags for single servings—something that can hold 2 to 3 cups of food (Rubbermaid makes a 2.2-gallon square container that can hold up to four days' worth of refrigerated food)

Owing to the sheer quantity of food I prepare, I generally must cook from morning to night while handling many other elements of being in business, such as locating specific ingredients and interacting with suppliers. These aspects of quality food preparation will not affect you to the same degree in your own home; nonetheless, there are a few things I've learned that can make your life as a dog food chef much simpler.

Protein

At Barker's Grub, we cook with a variety of meats, fish, and eggs. Each recipe is built around the source of protein. For the most part, these core ingredients are interchangeable from meal to meal; however, I rarely substitute veal, pork, or tuna. I don't use veal because of the way the animals are treated. I worry that tuna may pick up heavy metals such as mercury. Fresh fish contains whatever has gone into the water, including dumped garbage, and unfortunately are more and more contaminated. The canned variety of tuna, on the other hand, just isn't as good as fresh. Pork is okay, but not my favorite. Nonetheless, I do include special recipes in Chapter 6 for tuna and pork.

It is important to cook meats well to kill certain microbes. Chicken may carry salmonella, for example, and pork can carry trichinosis. Toxoplasmosis is a microscopic parasite that can contaminate beef and lamb, and cause illness in humans, even affecting developing fetuses. In dogs, it is thought that toxoplasmosis might also be acquired through contaminated soil and feces, exposure to which of course we cannot protect a dog. If your dog is sick in any way, do not give it raw meat. It is essential to take sanitary precautions when preparing meats for your dog. When handling food, thoroughly wash the cutting boards, surfaces, and utensils, and scrub your hands and fingernails.

Here is a list of proteins commonly found in my recipes:
- Beef
- Chicken (including hearts, liver, and gizzards)
- Eggs
- Fish: salmon, tilapia, mackerel, etc.
- Lamb
- Turkey
- Cottage cheese

You can use any cuts of meat for my recipes. In fact, I recommend that you buy whatever is on sale at the market and freeze some for later. Save yourself some money! Cooking at home can, and should, be economical.

Make friends with your local butcher. Since humankind's best friend was domesticated some fourteen thousand years ago, this beautiful, loving, and loyal animal has lived a rather unnatural, or should I say humanized, lifestyle. Because dogs no longer hunt for their meals, they never have the chance to experience chewing on fresh meat and bones. Therefore it is up to you, as a responsible pet lover, to pay a visit to your local butcher and shop for quality meats, as well as some goodies like marrow bones.

Keep in mind to ask your butcher for free-range chickens. This will ensure that you get the highest quality. "Free range" means not only that the chicken is being given organic feed and roaming in a huge pen, the pen is also clean, well maintained, and shared by only a few chickens. The definition of "organic" and "free range" on a label may vary from food product to food product because currently these terms are not regulated; however, products with these labels are still a better bet than any other-labeled meat. If you have a local farm that purports to keep their animals free range, it may be easy to verify their practices with a little investigation.

Produce and Supplements

Take the time to familiarize yourself with your local health food store and farmer's market. These are usually the best sources of high-quality vegetables, fruits, and nutritional supplements in a given community.

THE BUTCHER'S TREAT: MARROW BONES

If you love your dog, instead of giving him rawhide the next time he begs for a treat, give him a marrow bone. I guarantee that you'll see a "smile" on his face, and you'll have the satisfaction of knowing you are giving your dog the best nutrition.

Dogs need marrow bones because they contain iron and minerals such as calcium. In fact, more minerals are found in the bones than in the flesh of animals. You may also find that your butcher is more than happy to give you the marrow bones for free. Most butchers cannot sell all of their meat supply by the end of the day, and they have to throw the bones out.

Preparing the marrow bones for your dog to chew on is very easy. Either boil them for a few minutes until they are no longer pink or microwave them for a couple of minutes on a high setting.

Keep in mind that most bones are prone to splintering once they are cooked. By cooking the bone, you are in effect removing the gelatin, thus making the bone more brittle and hazardous to your pet's health. As a safety measure, always remove bones from your dog after a few hours, because over time they harden and may splinter.

To further ensure that you're giving your dog the best in food quality, cook with organically grown produce to avoid pesticides and other chemicals. If organic foods are exorbitantly

HOW TO WASH PRODUCE

It is important to wash fruits and vegetables thoroughly to remove pesticides, wax, dirt, bacteria, and so on. Because we cook with the peels on, this is doubly important—the peels contain so many nutrients. Wash organics as well as nonorganically grown produce to remove soil and remnants from transportation.

Use a small amount of dishwashing liquid. There are some brands that are biodegradable and that do not use animal testing, such as Ecover, available in health food stores and some major supermarket chains. The brand doesn't really matter, however, as this product will wash off in tap water.

You can also use citrus fruits for their acidity, such as lemons or oranges. Cut a lemon in two and rub its juices over the surface of the produce. Then rinse it under the tap. There is one product, called Citracelle, designed specifically for this purpose.

You can use a soft brush or your fingers to loosen debris. Run the surface of the produce under cool running water for a couple of minutes. Spinach, broccoli, watercress, and other leafy greens should be soaked for five minutes before rinsing under tap water. Don't use soap with leafy greens because it is hard to wash off afterwards.

expensive in your area, use those fresh ingredients you can buy at a good supermarket; just be extra sure to wash them thoroughly. (By supporting your local organic farmers, you may ultimately help bring down the cost of organic produce.)

These are some of the vegetables with which I cook:

- Broccoli
- Carrots
- Kale
- Kelp
- Peas
- Potatoes
- Pumpkin
- Squash
- String beans
- Sweet potatoes or yams
- Zucchini

Caution: Do not use potatoes that are sprouting or have turned green. Potatoes are a member of the nightshade family, which includes eggplants and bell peppers, as well as other, toxic plants, such as deadly nightshade. The green color and sprouts on potatoes indicate the presence of a low-level poison that will make a pooch feel under the weather. It is not lethal, but it is not great for your dog's health, either.

Fruits are most often found in my treat recipes, rather than the main courses. These are a few of my favorites:

- Apples
- Avocadoes
- Bananas
- Peaches
- Pears
- Tomatoes

Common seasonings include:
- Catnip (yes, even for a dog!)
- Dill
- Garlic
- Oregano
- Parsley

Some of the nutrients you should be giving your dog on a daily basis may be found only in a health food store. These include flaxseed oil (B and fatty acids), kelp (iron, iodine, phosphorus, chlorophyll, magnesium), and calcium powder. Check the Resources section at the back of this book to locate mail-order suppliers. Supplements are added to some of the Barker's Grub recipes, and these are explained in Chapter 3, which also includes recipes for making your own.

Staples

Here's a list of staples that you should always keep handy in your pantry. These are used over and over again in Barker's Grub recipes:
- Barley
- Flaxseed oil
- Molasses
- Pasta: elbow macaroni, spaghetti, etc.
- Oatmeal, either regular or instant
- Olive oil
- Peanut butter
- Rice, either brown or white
- Salmon oil

With only a few of these common ingredients, you can whip up a quick healthy meal for your dog in a matter of minutes. In

Chapter 6, I give my favorite dog food recipes and show how to improvise your own recipes from what you keep on hand in the kitchen.

The Rotation Diet and Transitioning to Whole Food

As a general rule of thumb, your dog's diet should consist of 50 percent protein from meat, 25 percent carbohydrates, and 25 percent vegetables. The recipes that I cook at Barker's Grub are all based on these ratios. Not only do my clients' dogs and my dogs, Hannah, Oscar, and George, love eating these meals, they are also thriving on them. Health and happiness are the ultimate goals of sound nutrition.

How Much, How Often

Generally, feeding your dog should in great part be based on breed, size, age, and how much exercise he or she receives. For example, if your dog is extremely active and is rather meager in weight, then perhaps his feeding portions should be increased to meet his nutritional needs. Conversely, the opposite should be done for a dog that is not getting enough exercise or is overweight—his feeding portions should be decreased. A dog is clearly too thin if the bones of his rib cage show through. Likewise, a dog is too heavy if you cannot feel his rib cage when you touch his side or his spine when you stroke the back. If you cannot determine this for yourself, your veterinarian can help you figure out if your pet is over- or underweight.

I encourage you to be flexible about these matters. Try to know your dog and exercise your common sense. Oftentimes I get quite irritated when I hear of a dog owner's reading the label on processed pet food and treating this information as if it were sent from God. The truth is that the feeding instructions on commercial pet foods are too general—they are purely suggestive. Every dog is different; therefore, no one uniform feeding schedule can apply to all dogs.

It is generally a good idea to give your dog as much food as it wants unless it has a weight problem. If you see that your dog is gaining weight, gradually cut back on its food. Vice versa, if you notice your dog is too thin, then increase its food slowly. You want to make subtle corrections in a diet, not drastic changes. And remember that overfeeding is not good dog keeping. Overfeeding also makes dog snacks, such as cookies, a sore issue. Most pet owners assume that they need to give cookies several times a day. Some dog owners go overboard and give treats almost every hour. Snacks are not a proper substitute for regular meals.

It is usually a good idea to feed your dog in small portions more than once a day. By spreading out your dog's meals over the course of the day, you help the dog maintain a higher metabolism. The thinking behind this is simple: whenever any animal eats, its body has to burn energy in order to break that food down. If you feed your dog its entire caloric and nutritional requirements in one heaping bowl, it is not going to take your dog as much energy to process the food. Try not to feed late in the evening when most of your dog's activity is done, though. (If you feed too late in the evening, you'll probably have to go for a walk in the middle of the night so your dog can relieve himself.) I feed Hannah, my oldest dog, twice a day owing to my work schedule—in the morning and in the evening—and I make sure that she gets plenty of good exercise every day.

An added benefit of feeding your dog in this fashion is that it can help reduce the risk of bloat, or gastric dilation, which is like colic in humans. This condition can be very uncomfortable and painful, or even deadly. Often, small portions of food spread over the course of a day can prevent bloat. This is especially relevant for larger breeds that have deep chests.

In the winter, animals require more calories and higher fat to keep warm. Dogs should not be shivering outside; they need body fat. So fat should either be added to the recipes or the meat you cook for them should be fatty meat. Don't trim it, especially if your dog spends a lot of time outdoors.

You can change the ratio of food components if the dog is becoming obese either by increasing the vegetables and decreasing the carbohydrates, or by slightly reducing the quantity at each feeding. I do not particularly like for people to reduce the quantity of food because oftentimes they go way overboard. You must not starve your dog.

What *Not* to Feed Your Dog

The most important food *not* to feed your dog is bones that splinter. *Chicken bones* top this list. Never, *ever* give your dog a chicken or turkey bone to gnaw on.

Rawhide also qualifies for a big *no*. In Chapter 1, I gave some reasons these chews are not good for your dog. I know many people feel their pooches love chews, and they don't want to deprive their animals. But take into account what ingredients go into them. While your pooch rips and tears at its favorite treat, that treat is virtually loaded with toxins and preservatives. Pigs' ears and bones basted in unnatural sauces should likewise be avoided. In addition, small pieces of rawhide chews can cause obstructions in your dog's intestines.

Have you ever questioned what goes into most *snack treats*? Why is it that they have such a long shelf life? The fact is that these snacks contain preservatives. Even three cookies a day can add up to a lot of preservatives during the course of a dog's life. Do not to overdose your pet with cookies—or anything else, for that matter. Remember: everything in moderation!

Chocolate is lethal to dogs. If you give them even a small quantity, you can kill them. Dogs have been known to start convulsing after eating fudge or boxed chocolate. *Don't* give them chocolate, and make sure they cannot get any on their own. If your dog eats chocolate, contact your veterinarian immediately.

Onions—whether fresh, cooked, powdered, or dehydrated— are also problematic, particularly for small dogs. You do not want to give onions to your dog in table scraps. According to Amy Marder, VDM, reporting in *Prevention* (1999), "The oil in onions is the culprit. It's an oxidant that affects hemoglobin, the substance that carries oxygen, in red blood cells." The resulting symptoms, such as anemia, rapid breathing, lethargy, vomiting, and heart murmur, may not appear for a day or more. If you suspect onion poisoning, contact your veterinarian immediately.

Lastly, *sugar* is not good for your pet. The dog does not require it. However, if your dog has a sweet tooth, give him or her dried fruit, such as figs, peaches, apricots, or banana chips—even slices of a whole fresh banana if she'll eat it (a good source of potassium). That should satisfy the "craving."

Transitioning to Home-Cooked Dog Food

The trick to weaning a dog off processed food is to do it slowly, over the course of a month. Reasons for caution are several. First, your dog likely has an emotional attachment to his previous food supply; he is accustomed to its flavor, smell, and texture. You want the transition to be as emotionally subtle as possible. Second, his digestive system may need time to adjust to the whole foods you are introducing into his diet, such as vegetables and grains. If you shift too rapidly, a dog may suffer from gas or diarrhea. You want the transition to be physically gentle. Lastly, if your dog has an unknown food allergy, by introducing new ingredients a few at a time you can observe their effects on your dog. You want to reduce the potential for harm.

When transitioning your dog to home-cooked food, keep your eye open for the following signs: vomiting, diarrhea, a duller coat over time (not a shinier one), lethargy, and gas. These indicate something is not going well, and you should consult your holistic veterinarian.

To make the transition to home-cooked food, don't remove all processed food at once. Start by mixing in small doses of homemade recipes with the dog's usual meals. Combine one-half cup of canned food with a couple of tablespoons of fresh food. Increase the amount of fresh food slowly, on every other day, likewise decreasing the canned food. Begin to give your dog more fresh wet food and less dry food. (As you already know, I consider dry food a scourge.)

It is important to start with a bland diet, such as chicken and rice, or beef and rice. In the first week, you'll add only the actual chicken and rice to the dog's diet. In weeks two and afterwards, you can begin to incorporate vegetables slowly. Here is a simple recipe:

Transitional Diet

Yield: 3 cups

Week One

1½ cups ground or cubed boneless chicken
2½ cups water
1½ cups cooked white rice

Boil the chicken in the water for approximately 30 to 45 minutes over low heat, until tender and white. Save the chicken broth for introducing vegetables into the diet later. (You can freeze and keep broth for up to 2 months.)

Combine the chicken and rice in a bowl, cool to room temperature, and serve.

Week Two

In the second week of your dog's transition, add one vegetable to the Transitional Diet. At the same time, continue to wean your dog off processed food, so that by the end of the second week you have finished the switch.

1½ cups ground or cubed boneless chicken
2½ cups water
1 cup cubed broccoli, zucchini, yellow squash, or green peas
1½ cups cooked white rice
1 to 2 heaping tablespoons gelatinous chicken broth (optional)

Boil the chicken in water for approximately 30 to 45 minutes over low heat, until tender and white. Drain and save broth separately to gel. Set chicken aside.

Boil the vegetables until soft and mushy, approximately 20 minutes.

Combine the chicken, rice, and vegetables in a bowl. Add 2 spoonfuls on top of the gelled broth. Cool to room temperature and serve.

Week Three

By now, your dog should be completely on the transitional food and off of processed food. During week three, keep increasing the amount of vegetables in the mix until they equal the amount of rice. As you add more vegetables, lessen the rice, until you are using ¾ cup of each.

Week Four

The amount of rice and vegetables should now be equal. You may use proportions of one or two different vegetables. The cooking instructions are the same as for week two.

Emotional Considerations

Are there any habitual attachments or other obstacles when transitioning your dog to home-cooked food? Not generally. Most dogs won't resist the switch. Home-cooked dog food tastes and smells better—plus, dogs adore real meat. If your dog is an exception, do not give up. You may need to cook the vegetables longer (dogs like them very soft), or add more broth for flavor.

Physical Adjustments

Unless the food is spoiled in some way, your dog should have no difficulty adjusting to the transition. However, some dogs react poorly to the chicken broth because of its richness. The high fat content may make their stools runny. To cope with diarrhea, simply cut back on the amount of broth until the dog's digestive tract begins to tolerate it. If this problem persists for more than two days, see your vet. It could be indicative of some other problem.

Allergies

Dogs may have an unidentified allergy to a specific ingredient. More commonly this is an allergy to a protein. To figure out which particular food is causing the problem, modify the recipe and try it again. For several feedings, change one ingredient and see if the situation improves.

Oftentimes, I get phone calls from customers and acquaintances making the food transition. Their most frequent question is: "Am I doing the right thing?" They believe in the miracle of modern science rather than age-old wisdom, and cannot see what is completely obvious.

Recently I got a telephone call from a lady who said, "Thank you, you saved my dog's life." She had phoned me two months earlier and told me she couldn't afford my catering services, although she understood their value. She told me the story of her seven-year-old husky who was undergoing chemotherapy for cancer and had lost a lot of weight. Her veterinarian had told her the dog was in danger. At the time, I gave her a simple cancer-healing recipe that she followed religiously.

Her veterinarian was amazed that the dog gained so much weight back so soon after chemotherapy, but I was not. I have seen it happen more than once. Among other benefits, home-cooked food is tempting for ill dogs. When they are nauseous, the smell of food must be enticing. Dogs start drooling the minute a meat aroma hits their noses.

When I hear stories like this one, I feel exhilarated. It makes me glad that people acknowledge the power of good nutrition.

So, when people ask me, "Am I doing the right thing?" I always answer, "Yes."

THE ROTATION DIET

The Rotation Diet is a simple way to ensure that your dog is being nourished with a broad range of nutrients. No one food can provide all the trace minerals and vitamins that are necessary for good health; therefore, no one food should compose the entire diet.

In the wild, animals eat what they can hunt or forage on a given day, every day consuming something different. Having evolved in harmony with the environment, their needs are generally met. It is only when they are deprived for many days or weeks of a specific nutrient that they develop a deficiency. One food source is richer in calcium or iron while another is high in vitamin C. As long as they have access to several food sources that complement and overlap each other nutritionally, they will be well fed. Nature contains variety and dogs must eat in variety. This is pure common sense.

What about domesticated dogs? In our desire to feed them well, isn't it more convenient and beneficial to give our dogs "perfectly" balanced meals out of the can? Wouldn't we be doing them a favor? The answer, of course, is no. The best possible way to ensure that our dogs' needs are met is to give them a variety of foods over a long period of time—essentially to mimic what occurs in nature. That way we can avoid nutritional deficiencies and hypersensitivity.

I often see dogs with food allergies and notice that they have been on an identical diet for years. Not only does it break my heart to imagine them eating the same thing day after day but it also is a sure way to build a food allergy. Sometimes dogs become hypersensitive in this scenario, meaning that some foods trigger an allergic response. That goes for home-cooked as well as processed dog foods. Whatever toxins may be present in a food build up in the body over time, provoking a greater and greater response and compromising the immune system. Instead, by offering different combinations of meats, vegetables, grains, and vitamin and mineral supplementation on a weekly or monthly basis, you can ensure your dog's optimal health and vitality.

At Barker's Grub we make weekly supplies of food for our customers. We work closely with customers to design rotational feeding menus that satisfy their pets' individual nutritional needs, taking into consideration taste preferences, size, age, genetics, health status, and sensitivities. The local holistic veterinarians refer their clients to me because the dogs have some kind of health problem that requires nutritional accommodation. In Chapter 6, I show how to prepare delicious and healthful recipes in both single serving and weekly versions. These same meals can be mixed and matched on a weekly or monthly basis, as in the sample Rotation Diets that follow here.

If your dog is hypersensitive, follow a weekly rotation. Hypersensitive animals should not be given the identical meal for more than two days in a row. Instead, skip the Monthly Rotation Diet and go straight to the Weekly Rotation Diet found on page 112.

There are a few things to keep in mind when planning your dog's personalized Rotation Diet. First, throughout any given month—and whether you are rotating meals daily or weekly—

at the end of each of the first three weeks, feed your dog a lower protein healing diet for one day. This gives the body a chance to catch up with itself. Once a month—let's say, on the last day of the fourth week—purify your dog by feeding him what I call the Purification Meal. This is a completely vegetarian meal that allows the body to detoxify, rest, and renew its organs and internal systems.

Most holistic veterinarians do not advocate complete fasting for purification. Fasting is too severe for domestic animals. Some dogs are so driven by habitual behavior, or they look forward with such great eagerness to mealtimes, that to deprive them of all food would be a severe punishment. Therefore, give them a healthful meal that has no protein and carbohydrates.

If you have determined that your dog requires a supplement—such as Healthy Powder, Eggshell Powder, or Kelp Substitute—double-check with your veterinarian to establish an appropriate supplementation schedule. Daily dosing of supplements is too frequent for most healthy dogs. A complete explanation of the supplements you should consider for your dog, and simple recipes for their home preparation are included in Chapter 3.

Warning

Oversupplementing with fat-soluble vitamins can be toxic. See Chapter 3 for more details.

Finally, no matter what meals you feed your dog and whichever diet plan you follow, provide plenty of fresh water; offer outdoor exercise; keep the dog's environment clean and sanitary; and give him love and affection. Your dog needs all these things to keep well.

These monthly and weekly Rotation Diets use the Barker's Grub recipes you will find in Chapter 6.

Never put a puppy or a pregnant or lactating female on the Purification Meal. They have a significant need for protein. If your dog has a chronic clinical ailment of any kind, consult a veterinarian before beginning this or any other diet.

Monthly Rotation Diet

Week One

Monday to Saturday: Main Dish—Moon Dog Mix
Sunday: Main Dish—Nonmeat Healing Diet

Week Two

Monday to Saturday: Main Dish—Juju Chicken and Rice
Sunday: Main Dish—Nonmeat Protein Healing Diet

Week Three

Monday to Saturday: Main Dish—Liver Love
Sunday: Main Dish—Nonmeat Protein Healing Diet

Week Four

Monday to Saturday Main Dish: Dodi Noodles with Lamb
Sunday: The Purification Meal

Weekly Rotation Diet

Week One

Monday: Moon Dog Mix
Tuesday: Moon Dog Mix
Wednesday: Juju Chicken and Rice

Thursday: Juju Chicken and Rice
Friday: Blue Moon Salmon Special
Saturday: Blue Moon Salmon Special
Sunday: Nonmeat Protein Healing Diet

Week Two

Monday: Sweet Woody
Tuesday: Sweet Woody
Wednesday: Dodi Noodles with Lamb
Thursday: Dodi Noodles with Lamb
Friday: Liver Love
Saturday: Liver Love
Sunday: Nonmeat Protein Healing Diet

Week Three

Monday: Winter Comfort Food
Tuesday: Winter Comfort Food
Wednesday: Rudy's Beet Stew
Thursday: Rudy's Beet Stew
Friday: Thanksgiving Dinner
Saturday: Thanksgiving Dinner
Sunday: Nonmeat Protein Healing Diet

Week Four

Monday: Aggression Reduction Meal
Tuesday: Aggression Reduction Meal
Wednesday: Halloween–Sam Hein Midnight Special
Thursday: Halloween–Sam Hein Midnight Special
Friday: Detox Italian Style
Saturday: Detox Italian Style
Sunday: The Purification Meal

Chapter 6

Barker's Grub Recipes

The Barker's Grub recipes are extensions of a basic recipe format that offers ample opportunities for variation and experimentation. Cook these first and then be inventive. The variations here are recipes I prepare most often and by popular demand for my customers. They are dishes their dogs and my own dogs have come to recognize and salivate over.

There is nothing difficult about my recipes. They have a wide margin for error and adaptation, and, in fact, the most convenient aspect of making dog food is that dogs eat almost anything. At least mine do. Even if you don't normally cook, I suspect that you will soon learn to whip up a menu for your pet using whatever ingredients are handy. Please don't forget that the most important ingredient is love. If you set aside an hour and a half on Sunday to make a batch of food for the week to come, that time may become a ritual of bonding between you and your companion animal. The aromas can fill the kitchen and lift your spirit.

When offered in rotation over a period of weeks, months, and years, the inherent balance of proteins, carbohydrates, and vegetables in these recipes keeps healthy dogs in excellent condition and improves the well-being of ailing animals. Several are indicated as "healing" recipes owing to their lower carbohydrate or lower protein content or high content of antioxidants. As recommended for the Rotation Diet in Chapter 5, all dogs can benefit once a week from a lessening of protein and once each month from a day of protein and carbohydrate purification. If you suspect your dog requires a special diet or has allergies and hypersensitivity, visit a holistic veterinarian. These veterinarians have additional training above and beyond ordinary vets, and they understand the intricacies of nutrition.

The Barker's Grub recipes in this chapter are single servings. Each recipe for a main dish is then followed by variations for the full-week version, as well as for substitutions of proteins, carbohydrates, and vegetables. That way, if your refrigerator contains chicken instead of turkey, and your pantry holds elbow macaroni instead of white rice, you can easily make an adjustment. Where no suggestion for a substitution has been made, it is because a change would tamper with the nutritional balance of the dish or might have a less than favorable impact on your dog's digestive tract. Some ingredients, for example, are too rich for dogs to tolerate well without rice to accompany them.

The recipes are divided into broths, puppy food, main dishes, healing recipes, and treats. Recipes for supplements can be found in Chapter 3.

BEFORE YOU BEGIN . . .

Fruits and Vegetables

Here are a few things to keep in mind when preparing fresh produce for Barker's Grub recipes:

- Do not peel fruits and vegetables; the peels contain vitamins and minerals. That includes potatoes or sweet potatoes or carrots. There are only two exceptions to this rule: bananas, for the most obvious reason, and yucca roots because they are barky and generally covered with inedible wax. I do not peel other roots, such as beets or turnips.

- Wash fruits and vegetables thoroughly. See How to Wash Produce (page 98).
- To cook vegetables, submerge them in water and boil until mushy. The timing varies according to the vegetable.
- Dogs don't chew their food much, so vegetables must already be somewhat broken down by boiling or steaming before they enter the digestive tract. Otherwise the dogs won't absorb their nutrients. Vegetables are particularly difficult because they contain so much fiber and cellulose. Nonetheless, dogs can tolerate vegetables when they are well cooked. The only vegetable that's okay given raw is the carrot, which in my recipes is grated. Carrots may also be cut into small sticks as a treat for dogs. If you discover your dog cannot tolerate raw carrots, just go back to cooking them.

General Notes

- Measure your ingredients as given in the recipe—most are for cooked ingredients. I specify cooked ingredients so that you have as many options as possible. You may be using instant rice; I may be using basmati rice. You may be using angel hair pasta; I may be using spaghetti number eight. The cooking instructions to accommodate every alternative would vary greatly.
- If this were a cookbook for human beings, I certainly could and would be more specific about ingredients and their preparation. Your dog probably doesn't care to the same degree. Likewise, it's not going to "ruin" the recipe

if you use a half-cup too much broccoli or one-quarter cup extra chicken liver. Your dog is going to be your most appreciative audience almost no matter what.

- Follow the instructions on the package to prepare rice, pasta, oatmeal, and barley, and so on. Most carbohydrates are available in several possible forms.
- Cook your rice, pasta, barley, oatmeal, and the like in broth to add both color and flavor to your main dishes.

Seasonal Adjustments

In warm-weather months (i.e., late spring, summer, and early autumn) reduce the fat content of recipes. Use leaner cuts of meat. Also reduce carbohydrates, especially pasta, and slightly increase the vegetable content.

During cold-weather months (i.e., late autumn, winter, and early spring) reverse the above instruction. Give your dogs more fatty cuts of meat, more carbohydrates, and slightly fewer vegetables so that they can keep warm by putting an added layer of fat on their bodies.

BROTHS

Chicken or Turkey Broth

Beef or Lamb Broth

Vegetable Broth

At the beginning of most of my recipes you will be asked to brown or boil your meat, and boil the vegetables. Broth is the liquid reserved from the boiling process. This broth can be added to main dishes as a final seasoning, or used to replace the water when preparing rice or pasta. The broth becomes a source of additional protein, vitamins, and minerals. When a dog is sick, it can often tolerate broth even if it cannot hold down solid foods.

Suggested Feeding for Adult Dogs

Size	Weight	Cups of Food per Day
Toy Breeds	2 to 10 lbs.	½ to 2
Small Breeds	10 to 35 lbs.	2 to 5½
Medium Breeds	35 to 60 lbs.	5½ to 7½
Large Breeds	60 to 90 lbs.	7½ to 9
Giant Breeds	90 to 160 lbs.	9 to 14

IMPORTANT: This chart is a general guideline. It should not be used to replace common sense.

Chicken or Turkey Broth

Yield: 3 cups
Preparation time: 25 minutes
Cooking time: 45 minutes

Follow this recipe for chicken or turkey broth when you make your general recipes.

1½ cups cubed chicken, or 1½ cups ground turkey,
  or 1½ cups chopped chickens hearts and livers
  (12 ounces)
2½ cups water

Boil the chicken or chicken parts in water for 45 minutes, the ground turkey for 30 minutes. Strain the meat from your liquid and refrigerate for use in other recipes. Reserve the broth in an airtight plastic container in the freezer. Or keep it in the refrigerator, where it will stay fresh for three or four days.

When the broth is cooled, it will become gelatinous, which actually makes it easy to spoon and measure. Yet it thaws and liquefies rapidly when spooned over heated ingredients.

Beef or Lamb Broth

Yield: 3 cups
Preparation time: 25 minutes
Cooking time: 45 minutes

Follow this recipe for beef or lamb broth when making your general recipes.

1½ cups ground or cubed beef, or 1½ cups ground or cubed lamb
2½ cups water

Boil the ground beef or lamb in water for 30 minutes, the cubed meat for 45 minutes, until tender.

Strain the meat from the liquid and refrigerate for use in other recipes. Reserve the broth in an airtight plastic container in the freezer or refrigerator.

Vegetable Broth

Whenever you boil vegetables for the main dishes, save the cooking water—that's a vegetable broth. Vegetable broths can add nutrients to your recipes when they are substituted for plain water.

Some vegetables produce very aromatic and colorful broths, such as beets. Beet broth looks like red wine. If you use vegetable broth for cooking rice, it becomes truly beautiful.

To create a vegetable broth, strain out the vegetable pulp after boiling (otherwise what you've got is soup) and store in refrigerator for future recipes.

PUPPY FOOD

Chicken Puppy Food

Beef Puppy Food

Turkey and Egg Puppy Food

Liver Puppy Food

Puppy food is essentially the same as adult dog food. Puppies eat the same ingredients but in a slightly different ratio: 60 percent protein, 20 percent carbohydrates, and 20 percent vegetables. The main distinction between puppy food and adult dog food is that it needs to be mushier because the puppies are teething and their gums are tender. Teething starts at around five weeks of age and continues until approximately three months, when the "milk teeth" fall out and adult teeth come in.

To make the puppy food appropriately mushy, prepare any of the main dish recipes and, at the last moment, put the ingredients into a food processor or blender and puree to the consistency of human baby food or apple sauce. You can also use a handheld masher, if necessary.

At first, while the puppy is still nursing, place a dab of puppy food on its paw and let it lick the food off to get used to it. As the puppy's teeth come in, leave it a bowl of food, and soon the young animal will make the switch. By two months a puppy is generally eating solid food. That's when you can stop mushing it up. Let it exercise its new teeth. (If you don't it will probably exercise them on material objects, such as your shoes and couch.)

Puppies should eat high-protein foods until eight or nine months of age or more, depending on the size and breed of dog. Some small breeds reach maturity sooner than larger breeds. Consult your veterinarian for advice on the subject. At some point, the dog will switch to adult dog food—50 percent protein.

Use any of the main-dish recipes modified as puppy food, or try the following four basic puppy food recipes for chicken, beef, turkey and eggs, and liver.

Chicken Puppy Food

Yield: 3½ cups, or 1 serving
Preparation time: 30 minutes
Cooking time: 30 minutes

2 cups ground or cubed chicken
½ cup green beans (fresh or frozen)
1 carrot, grated
1 cup cooked white or brown rice
1 tablespoon plain yogurt

Boil the chicken for 20 minutes. Drain. Reserve broth for
    another use. Set chicken aside.
Boil the green beans until they are soft, approximately
    20 minutes.
Combine the chicken, beans, carrot, and rice in a dog bowl.
    Stir in the yogurt.
Serve at room temperature.

Variation

Full-Week Recipe

14 cups ground or cubed chicken
3½ cups green beans
7 carrots, grated
7 cups cooked white or brown rice
7 tablespoons plain yogurt

Beef Puppy Food

Yield: 3½ cups, or 1 serving
Preparation time: 30 minutes
Cooking time: 30 minutes

2 cups ground or cubed beef (1 pound)
1 tablespoon olive oil
¾ cup pasta (any kind of noodles will do)
½ cup cubed sweet potatoes
¼ cup green peas (fresh or frozen)
1 tablespoon grated Parmesan cheese

Brown the beef in the olive oil in a skillet over low heat for approximately 20 minutes, until the meat is thoroughly cooked.

Boil the pasta according to the directions on the package.

Boil the sweet potatoes for 25 minutes, until very mushy.

Boil the green peas for 20 minutes, or until very soft.

Combine the meat and vegetables in a dog food bowl. Sprinkle with Parmesan cheese. Serve at room temperature.

Variation

Full-Week Recipe

14 cups ground or cubed beef (7 pounds)
¼ cup olive oil
5¼ cups cooked pasta
3½ cups cubed sweet potatoes
1¾ cups green peas
¼ cup grated Parmesan cheese

Turkey and Egg Puppy Food

Yield: 3½ cups, or 1 serving
Preparation time: 30 minutes
Cooking time: 30 minutes

2 cups ground or cubed turkey (1 pound)
3 or 4 large eggs
1 tablespoon olive oil
¼ cup chopped broccoli
¾ cup cooked oatmeal

Boil the turkey for approximately 20 to 25 minutes. Drain.
   Reserve broth for another use.
Set turkey aside.
Scramble the eggs in a skillet with the olive oil. Set aside.
Boil the broccoli for approximately 25 minutes, or until
   very soft.
Combine all the ingredients in a dog dish and serve at room
   temperature.

Variation

Full-Week Recipe

14 cups ground or cubed turkey (7 pounds)
2½ dozen large eggs
¼ cup olive oil
1¾ cups chopped broccoli
5¼ cups cooked oatmeal

Liver Puppy Food

Yield: 3½ cups, or 1 serving
Preparation time: 30 minutes
Cooking time: 30 minutes

You will need skewers for this recipe, which must be prepared over an open flame, on either a gas stove or a grill. You may want to save this recipe for a day when you plan to barbecue.

2 cups chopped chicken livers
½ cup sliced zucchini
1 cup cooked white rice

Place the chicken livers on skewers. Sear them over an open flame, turning every 15 seconds, until the outsides are browned, approximately 2 to 3 minutes.

Boil the zucchini for approximately 25 minutes, or until mushy.

Combine all the ingredients in a dog dish and serve at room temperature.

Main Dishes

Moon Dog Mix: Beef and Potato

Dodi Noodles with Lamb

Juju Chicken and Rice

Sweet Woody: Turkey, Oatmeal, and Sweet Potatoes

Blue Moon Salmon Special

Halloween—Sam Hein Midnight Special

Thanksgiving Dinner

Easter Recipe

Tuna Togetherness

Lo Mein Barking Style

The Purification Meal

Barker's Grub

Moon Dog Mix: Beef and Potato

Yield: 3 cups, or 1 serving
Preparation time: 10 minutes
Cooking time: 45 minutes

Moon Dog was my very first dog food client, and he has always loved all my recipes, even the experimental ones. He's part wolf—a real macho dog—and I wanted to feed him a substantial meal. This versatile beef and potato recipe is named in his honor because he is still my best and most loyal customer. His mama is a good friend, too, and has spent hours of time hanging out with me in the kitchen.

1½ cups extra-fatty ground or cubed beef
    (12 ounces)
2 tablespoons olive oil
1½ cups cubed potatoes
1 strip bacon, cooked and coarsely chopped
1 tablespoon dill, fresh or dried
2 tablespoons grated Parmesan cheese

Brown the beef in the olive oil in a large skillet over low heat, making sure not to overcook it. (In other words, it should remain a little pink inside.) To eliminate bacteria, meat must be cooked until it reaches 180 degrees Fahrenheit inside and outside. You can check internal temperature with a meat thermometer if you doubt that you have done so. Browning will take approximately 20 to 30 minutes if the meat is not frozen; otherwise it will take longer. Stir frequently. (If you choose, you can boil the meat instead of

browning it. That way it will be brown inside and out. To
boil, follow the beef broth recipe on page 121.)

Boil the potatoes until they are tender, approximately 20 to
30 minutes. Drain in a colander.

Mix the beef, potatoes, bacon, and dill in a bowl, sprinkle
with Parmesan cheese, and serve the Moon Dog Mix to
your pooch.

Variations

Full-Week Recipe

> 10½ cups ground or cubed beef (5 pounds)
> ½ cup olive oil
> 10½ cups cubed potatoes
> 7 strips bacon
> ¼ cup dill, fresh or dried
> grated Parmesan cheese

Protein: You may substitute lamb, chicken, or turkey for the
beef in the same quantities. For the one-serving meal, use 1½
cups; for the full-week variation, use 10½ cups.

Carbohydrates: 1½ cups cooked barley may be substituted for
the potatoes.

Vegetables: You can add any kind of vegetable to the mix,
bringing the ratio of nutrients to 50% protein, 25% carbohydrate, and 25% vegetable. Increase the amount of beef in the
recipe to 2 cups and decrease the potatoes to 1 cup. When boiling the vegetables, just toss them in for 20 minutes with the
potatoes. I recommend that you add 1 cup sliced zucchini, 1 cup
grated carrots, or 1 cup chopped carrots.

Dodi Noodles with Lamb

Yield: 3 cups, or 1 serving
Preparation time: 10 minutes
Cooking time: 30 minutes

This aromatic recipe is named after my second dog, George. Don't ask me how I came up with that pet name "Dodi," but George loves noodles—especially spaghetti! (Dodi is my special little noodle.) I make this dish with elbow macaroni because they are so easy to measure in a cup. It's also very attractive and smells good—so good in fact that when my friend Caroline came over she wanted to eat a bowl herself.

1½ cups extra-fatty ground or cubed lamb meat
    (1 pound)
2 tablespoons olive oil (for browning)
¾ cup elbow macaroni
¾ cup green peas, frozen and thawed, or fresh, if
    you can get them
1 tablespoon plain yogurt
1 tablespoon fresh Chinese parsley (cilantro), finely
    chopped

Boil the meat or brown the lamb meat in the olive oil in a large skillet over low heat, making sure not to overcook it, approximately 30 to 40 minutes. Stir frequently. If boiling, drain meat and reserve broth for another use. Set meat aside.
Boil the elbow macaroni at the same time until tender, approximately 12 minutes.

Boil the green peas according to the directions on the package. Thoroughly mix the meat, macaroni, and other ingredients in a large bowl. Serve.

Variations

Full-Week Recipe

> 10½ cups ground or cubed lamb meat (5 pounds)
> ½ cup olive oil
> 5¾ cups elbow macaroni
> 5¾ cups green peas
> ¼ cup fresh Chinese parsley, finely chopped

Protein: If you want a lower fat version, try boneless turkey breast. Boil the breast for approximately half an hour and then cut it in ¼-inch cubes. Boiling actually lessens the fat content of the recipe even more.

Carbohydrates: You can substitute either white or brown rice for the noodles if you prefer. And you can use different shape pasta, such as spaghetti. I break spaghetti noodles in half when I cook them because they fit better in the pot. Dogs can pretty much chow down on any size of noodle—length does not deter or hinder them.

Vegetables: Because they are complex carbohydrates, you can substitute pumpkin or other squash for the noodles. They are starches and have a high sugar content. Another vegetable to substitute for the green peas would be asparagus.

Juju Chicken and Rice

Yield: 3 cups, or 1 serving
Preparation time: 10 minutes
Cooking time: 40 minutes

This juicy recipe is named after my third dog, Oscar, who is affectionately known as "Juju," meaning magic. You see, Oscar had parvovirus as a pup, and it is a true miracle that he survived.

This tasty recipe was the first I ever tried on Oscar when he was recovering. The rice was especially important in his healing diet because he had chronically loose bowels. It balanced out that virtually unmentionable problem. Most important, he loved the flavor!

1½ cups cubed chicken (1 pound)
2 tablespoons olive oil (for browning)
½ cup chopped green vegetables (green peas,
    broccoli, zucchini, celery, or asparagus)
1½ cups cooked rice, brown or white
2 tablespoons crumbled feta cheese
2 garlic cloves, minced
2 tablespoons dill, dried or fresh

Brown or boil the chicken meat. If browning, put meat in a
    skillet with the olive oil and cook over low heat for about
    30 minutes. Stir frequently. If boiling, cover with water
    and cook for 30 to 45 minutes. Drain the chicken and
    reserve broth for another use. Set meat aside.
Boil or steam the vegetables until they are tender to the bite,
    but not limp; time varies with the vegetable. Combine the

chicken, vegetables, and rice in a mixing bowl; then stir in the feta cheese, garlic, and dill. Serve.

Variations

Full-Week Recipe

10½ cups cubed chicken (5 pounds)
½ cup olive oil
3½ cups chopped vegetables
10½ cups cooked rice
½ cup crumbled feta cheese
14 garlic cloves
½ cup dill, dried or fresh

Protein: Any kind of meat may be substituted for the chicken. Lamb or beef work equally well; use 1½ cups.

Carbohydrates: A version that is also very good for recovery is barley. Barley is gentle on the stomach; it's like boiled porridge. It soothes the nerves and has a lot of fiber in it. Substitute 1½ cups of cooked barley for the rice.

Vegetables: In the autumn, use 1 cup of cooked butternut squash, pumpkin, or any other winter squash for your vegetable selection instead of green vegetables.

Sweet Woody:
Turkey, Oatmeal, and Sweet Potatoes

Yield: 3 cups, or 1 serving
Preparation time: 10 minutes
Cooking time: 20 minutes

I decided to name this recipe after a rescue puppy I fostered, a Red Bone–Coonhound mix that I named Woody because he was the color of orange-brown wood. This recipe is the same color, and almost as sweet as Woody's nature.

1½ cups cubed or ground turkey (12 ounces)
2 tablespoons olive oil (for browning)
¾ cup cubed sweet potatoes, with skins
¾ cups cooked oatmeal (either traditional or instant)
2 tablespoons cottage cheese
1 garlic clove, minced

Brown the turkey meat in olive oil in a large skillet over low heat, stirring often, approximately 30 to 40 minutes, or boil it for 30 minutes, covered, in a pot of water. Drain and reserve broth for another use. Set turkey aside.

Meanwhile, boil the sweet potatoes for 20 to 25 minutes, until tender, and drain.

Combine the turkey, sweet potatoes, oatmeal, and cottage cheese in a mixing bowl with the garlic. Serve.

Variations

Full-Week Recipe

        10½ cups cubed turkey (5 pounds)
        ½ cup olive oil
        5¾ cups cubed sweet potatoes
        5¾ cups cooked oatmeal
        ½ cup cottage cheese
        7 garlic cloves

Protein: You can substitute chicken for the turkey.

Vegetables: For sweet potatoes, you can substitute white potatoes.

Blue Moon Salmon Special

Yield: 3 cups, or 1 serving
Preparation time: 5 minutes
Cooking time: 20 minutes

This recipe is called the "Blue Moon" special because I serve salmon to my dogs only once in a blue moon. At my house salmon is reserved for occasions such as birthdays and holidays. You can make this dish with any kind of fish, however, and I recommend that you serve variations of it frequently, so that your dog will reap the benefit of those wonderful omega-3 fatty acids.

What's really special about this recipe is the way that the fish and eggs are mixed together. The smell is absolutely putrid, but dogs love it—I swear!

1 dozen large eggs
½ cup cooked rice, white or brown
1 cup shredded smoked salmon (8 ounces)
½ cup cooked green peas or steamed chopped
    asparagus
2 tablespoons dill, dried or fresh

Hard-boil the eggs and remove the shells. Reserve the eggshells
    to make Eggshell Powder recipe (see page 75).
Put the eggs, rice, and salmon in a mixing bowl and stir
    together until they form a paste. Add the vegetable and dill,
    and thoroughly mix. Serve.

Variations

> 7 dozen large eggs
> 3½ cups cooked rice, white or brown
> 7 cups shredded smoked salmon
> 3½ cups cooked peas or chopped asparagus
> ½ cup dill, dried or fresh

Protein: You can use any boneless fish in place of the smoked salmon. Steam or boil fish filets of mackerel or tilapia, for example.

Halloween—Sam Hein Midnight Special

Yield: 3 cups, or 1 serving
Preparation time: 1 hour 10 minutes
Cooking time: 35 minutes

This is a hearty fall meal and there's no way to screw it up.

For an annual bash at my home on Halloween, I prepare pumpkin bread, pumpkin squares, pumpkin pie, and pumpkin cookies for our four-legged friends. People know that they can bring their dogs to my house as members of the party. My only requirement is that all the animals be dressed in costume.

This year Hannah, my Shepherd-Collie mix, was a housemaid, wearing an apron and kerchief on her head. George, my smaller Terrier, was her mop. Oscar was Dracula—he wore a cape over his luminescent Black Lab–Doberman fur. Oscar seemed scary to me, but many of my guests said he looked like Batman.

1½ cups ground chicken (12 ounces)
2 tablespoons olive oil
¾ cup green peas
¾ cup mashed cooked pumpkin

Brown the chicken in the olive oil in a large skillet over low heat for approximately 30 minutes. Stir frequently. Do not overcook.

Boil the peas for approximately 5 minutes, or use them raw—either is okay.

Combine the meat, peas, and pumpkin in a bowl. Serve.

Variations

Full-Week Recipe

       10½ cups ground chicken (5 pounds)
       ½ cup olive oil
       5¾ cups green peas
       5¾ cups mashed cooked pumpkin

Thanksgiving Dinner

***

Yield: 3 cups, or 1 serving
Preparation time: 40 minutes
Cooking time: 45 minutes

Remember, you can feed your dog whatever you are eating. So, if you find it hard to make separate meals, never fear! Make whatever you're eating and set some aside for your dog. A meal like Thanksgiving Dinner is easy. This recipe is a variation on what we serve during our favorite American celebration.

1½ cups ground or cubed turkey (12 ounces)
2 tablespoons olive oil
¾ cup sliced string beans
¾ cup mashed sweet potatoes
½ teaspoon ground cinnamon (optional: your dog
  may dislike it)

Brown the turkey in the olive oil in a large skillet over low heat
  for 30 to 45 minutes. Stir frequently.
Boil the string beans until they are tender but not yet mushy,
  about 20 minutes.
Add the turkey and string beans to the mashed sweet potatoes
  in a bowl and stir well. Stir in the cinnamon and serve.

Variations

Full-Week Recipe

10½ cups ground or cubed turkey (5 pounds)
½ cup olive oil

5¾ cups mashed sweet potatoes
5¾ cups sliced string beans
3½ teaspoons ground cinnamon (optional)

Carbohydrates: You may substitute regular mashed potatoes or mashed turnips.

Vegetables: You may use Brussels sprouts for the string beans.

Easter Recipe

Yield: 3 cups, or 1 serving
Preparation time: 5 minutes
Cooking time: 40 minutes

Every time I cook eggs for breakfast I can see my dogs drooling. They gather at my feet and their eyes shift back and forth from me to my pots and pans. Of course, I share whatever I make with them. This Easter Recipe was created so that all my clients would have an easy egg meal to feed their dogs.

6 large eggs
2 tablespoons olive oil
¾ cup mashed potatoes
¾ cup green peas (raw or cooked)
1 tablespoon fresh dill or parsley, finely chopped

Crack the eggs into a bowl and reserve the shells to make Eggshell Powder (see page 75). Beat the eggs with a fork, making sure the whites and yolks are thoroughly mixed.

Grease a large skillet with the olive oil and pour the eggs into it. Cook over low heat, continuously scrambling, until eggs are fully cooked and hold together, about 7 minutes.

Combine the eggs, potatoes, peas, and herb in a bowl. Mix well, let cool, and serve at room temperature.

Variations

Full-Week Recipe

3½ dozen large eggs

½ cup olive oil

5¾ cups mashed potatoes

5¾ cups green peas

¼ cup fresh dill or parsley, finely chopped

Tuna Togetherness

Yield: 3 cups, or 1 serving
Preparation time: 10 minutes
Cooking time: 35 minutes

*Tuna is one of those foods my animals are fed rarely. They love it,
but I prefer to give them fresh steaks instead of canned fish and the
steaks are expensive. Since I live with cats as well as dogs, I developed a recipe they all could enjoy—even something I would like. At
my house, all creatures, the two-legged as well as the four-legged,
often sit down to meals together.*

3 6-ounce cans water-packed tuna or 1¼ pounds
    fresh tuna steak
2 tablespoons olive oil (for fresh tuna)
¾ cup cubed potatoes
¾ cup chopped celery
2 tablespoons dill, fresh or dried

If using tuna steak, brown the fish in the olive oil in a large
    skillet and cook thoroughly, approximately 10 minutes.
    You will find that the steaks fall apart before you are
    through. That's fine. Place in a large mixing bowl. If
    using canned tuna, just open the can and put it into the
    mixing bowl.
Boil the potatoes until soft, about 10 minutes. Boil the celery
    until soft, about 5 minutes.
Add the potatoes and celery to the tuna, stir well, add dill,
    and cool to room temperature. Serve.

Variations

Full-Week Recipe

> 21 6-ounce cans water-packed tuna or 8¾
>   pounds fresh tuna
> ½ cup olive oil
> 5¼ cups cubed potatoes
> 3½ cups chopped celery
> ½ cup dill, fresh or dried

Lo Mein Barking Style

Yield: 3¼ cups, or 1 serving
Preparation time: 10 minutes
Cooking time: 30 minutes

One night I got Chinese takeout. Of course, my dogs were panting and drooling and begging and pleading for a taste, so after I was finished I gave them my leftovers. A couple of hours later, we all came down with a major case of the runs.

That's when I decided what we really needed was a recipe that resembled Chinese food without unwanted aftereffects—something that didn't have so many sauces and spices, but offered the combination of meat and vegetables over rice noodles. Lo Mein Barking Style is the solution.

> 1½ cups ground or cubed chicken breast
>   (12 ounces) or ground or cubed beef
> 2 tablespoons olive oil
> ¾ cup rice noodles
> ½ cup grated carrots
> ½ cup green peas
> 3 tablespoons chicken or beef broth (see page 120 or 121)

Brown the chicken or beef in the olive oil in a skillet over low heat for 30 minutes, or until meat is cooked through.
Boil the rice noodles until tender, approximately 12 minutes. Cook the carrots and peas until soft. Mix the chicken, noodles, and vegetables in a large bowl. Top with the chicken broth, let cool, and serve at room temperature.

Variations

Full-Week Recipe

10½ cups ground or cubed chicken or beef
   (5 pounds)
½ cup olive oil
5¼ cups rice noodles
3½ cups grated carrots
3½ cups green peas
¾ cup chicken or beef broth

The Purification Meal

Yield: 3 cups, or 1 serving
Preparation time: 10 minutes
Cooking time: 10 minutes

Feed your dog this vegetarian meal once at the end of each month to give its body a chance to purify itself. Skip the morning feeding and give this as a replacement for the evening main dish. Your dog doesn't have to miss an entire day of eating, just take a break from protein and carbohydrates. Our canine companions so look forward to food that if you didn't give them a placebo they would feel very deprived. My dogs happen to enjoy this meal on its own merits anyway.

The lymphatic system is a major component of the immune system. The lymph fluid carries white blood cells through the body to combat invading bacteria and remove damaged cells. You can assist the functioning of the lymph nodes by detoxifying your dog. Feed the dog plenty of leafy green vegetables and tomatoes.

Note: Check with your veterinarian if your dog is ill before detoxifying it. Dogs that are sick must receive adequate nutrition. Pregnant and lactating females and puppies should not be fed the Purification Meal. Their need for high-energy carbohydrates is significant, and protein is essential for building a fetal pup or newborn pup.

2 cups assorted green vegetables, boiled or steamed
(especially zucchini or broccoli)
1 cup plain yogurt

Combine the vegetables and yogurt in a bowl and serve with
   plenty of fresh water alongside.

HEALING RECIPES

Liver Love

Winter Comfort Food

Low-Fat Heart Food

Davie's Juicy Jiggly-Wiggly Anemia Diet

Weight-Loss Recipe

Nonmeat Protein Healing Diet

Colitis Diet

TNT Constipation Recipe

Anti-Cancer Food

Kidney Healing Meal

Aggression Reduction Meal

Arthritis Be Gone

Barker's Grub

Diabetes Meal

Rudy's Beet Stew

Detox Italian Style

Food has the incredible power to maintain and restore health. It fuels every physiological system and is therefore the body's closest ally in the prevention of and recovering from disease. This is also why a poor diet can lead, over time, to disastrous consequences. When a dog is not receiving the required vitamins, minerals, and other essential nutrients, there may be a cascade effect of lowered immunity followed by ill health.

There is a growing consensus among holistic veterinarians that most canine ailments can be traced in some way to nutritional deficiencies. Holistic veterinarian Grace Calabrese concurs and adds, "None of the therapies I use will have maximum effect if the animal is not already on a good diet." Not only does improper nutrition sabotage optimal health, it limits the body's innate ability to recuperate. If you want your dog to thrive, you must feed it well.

Preventive Nutrition

Preventing physical ailments is not always easy, and different breeds have different susceptibilities to disease. Since your beloved dog is dependent on you, it is worth educating yourself as to how best to help, and one place to start learning is on the Internet, where there are numerous breed-specific Web sites. See the Resources section at the back of the book for suggestions.

The books *Dr. Pitcairn's Complete Guide to Natural Health for Dogs and Cats,* by Richard H. Pitcairn and Susan Hubble Pitcairn, and *Earl Mindell's Nutrition and Health for Dogs,* by Earl Mindell and Elizabeth Renaghan, both offer breed-specific lists detailing health tendencies. Mixed-breed dogs generally have fewer congenital problems than do pure breeds.

While knowing to which kind of ailments your dog may be prone is a good first step, ultimately you will need expert advice on how to manage these problems. In the meantime, it is easily within your capability to build a solid nutritional foundation that supports your dog's general health. Veterinarian Leslie Taylor of the Canal Clinic in Potomac, Maryland, says, "Practicing preventive medicine is practicing preventive nutrition; you cannot possibly go or do wrong by having your dog on a proper diet." The Rotation Diet outlined in Chapter 5 ensures that your dog gets the right nutrients in a balanced diet.

Holistic veterinarians look for and remove obstacles to health so that the body can and will employ its own recuperative powers. Food is not the answer to every problem; nonetheless, a poor diet is an obstacle to healing. Holistic veterinarians routinely advocate homemade food for their canine patients. Dr. Calabrese says, "The first thing to do is put the dog on a fresh whole-food diet, even before the first appointment. Over the years I have discovered, to my initial surprise, that by the time an appointment comes up the problem is either completely gone or has dramatically improved."

Dr. Monique Maniet, a holistic veterinarian at Veterinary Holistic Care in Bethesda, states, "I work with acupuncture, Chinese herbs, or homeopathy. In addition, I may also recommend specific dietary modifications and supplements, and I look closely at lifestyle issues, such as how much or little exercise a dog is taking and its environment. I always prefer noninvasive methods to surgery and drugs." Furthermore, she adds, "Whatever conditions my patients are experiencing, the first thing I tackle is their food, which I immediately change to homemade."

There is an added benefit: home cooking is the most therapeutic medicine I know, because love is the true healer of ailments and the best immune-system booster and protector. Savory aromas wafting from the kitchen and throughout the house, kind words spoken as food is placed in the bowl, and the gentle touch of a hand on your dog's head as it comes to eat all communicate love. In addition to the wholesome and nutritious ingredients you have selected, the caring energy that you pour into your dog's food makes it potent. Food you cook with your hands is an extension of your loving presence and intentions.

Dr. Michael W. Fox tells me that his three dogs always know when he is cooking their food, as distinct from preparing his own meal. "It's not just that I'm a vegetarian, and what I cook for them includes animal protein, so they can smell the difference. I tell them it's time to cook their food for the week and they sit around the kitchen imbuing it with an ambiance of relaxed and joyful anticipation."

Restorative Nutrition

Many illnesses and physical conditions can be cured—or at least managed—by taking nutritional measures. Kidney disease mandates lowered protein consumption, for example. A veterinarian can help you figure out what is appropriate for your individual dog. Sometimes nutritional measures are useful as adjuncts to other treatments, such as surgery or chemotherapy. The practices of conventional medicine, while often life saving, can also traumatize a dog's body. With wholesome food you can help soothe your savaged beast.

Ideally, nutrition should be a long-term health strategy, not a form of emergency medicine. The fifteen recipes that follow are the ones most commonly requested by Barker's Grub clients for their dogs.

Liver Love

———

Yield: 3 cups, or 1 serving
Preparation time: 20 minutes
Cooking time: 30 minutes

Liver is a marvelous source of natural iron, which is beneficial for anemic animals or those recovering from surgical procedures such as neutering or spaying. In fact, most organ meats have concentrated essential nutrients. My mother's dog Bianca was spayed and lost a lot of blood during the procedure. Her vet said it would take at least ten days for Bianca to regain complete mobility and pep. Fed this diet of liver, however, she was jumping up and down within three days.

An added benefit: If you keep cats as well as dogs, both creatures will enjoy this recipe, and it is high in taurine, which is good for cats' hearts.

1½ cups chicken livers
2 tablespoons olive oil
¾ cup cooked white rice
¾ cup mashed cooked carrots
    (about 3 medium carrots)
1 tablespoon yogurt (optional)
1 tablespoon dried catnip

Brown the chicken livers in the olive oil in a skillet over low heat for approximately 20 minutes. Do not overcook (if overcooked, the livers become extremely dry).
Combine the livers, rice, carrots, and yogurt in a bowl with the catnip, making sure to blend well. Serve.

Variations

10½ cups chicken livers (5 pounds)
½ cup olive oil
5¾ cups cooked white rice
5¾ cups mashed cooked carrots
    (10 to 12 medium carrots)
¼ cup yogurt (optional)
7 tablespoons dried catnip

Protein: You may substitute chicken hearts for chicken livers, or use a combination of half and half of each.

Carbohydrates: Organ meats are nutritious and extremely rich, therefore I do not recommend substituting any other carbohydrate for the rice. Rice balances out the richness of the organ meats, which some dogs may find interferes with digestion. Rice prevents diarrhea.

Vegetables: You may substitute sweet potatoes or another complex carbohydrate for the carrots in the same quantity. If you want a meal especially full of iron for an anemic dog or one recovering from surgery, substitute broccoli in the same proportions.

Winter Comfort Food

Yield: 3 cups, or 1 serving
Preparation time: 45 minutes
Cooking time: 45 minutes

At the start of cold weather, I get in the mood for comfort food. There is something very appealing about this earthy meal; it soothes the spirit and boosts the immune system. Winter Comfort Food is particularly good if your dog has developed kennel cough from being boarded around sick animals, or if you just adopted a shelter dog and want to treat or prevent an upper-respiratory infection.

1½ cups ground or cubed beef (12 ounces)
2 tablespoons olive oil
¾ cup cooked barley
¾ cup cubed turnips
½ teaspoon ground cinnamon (optional: some
    dogs may dislike it)

Brown the meat in the olive oil in a large skillet over low heat for approximately 30 minutes, or until cooked through.
Boil the barley until it is soft.
Boil the turnips until they are tender, about 5 minutes.
Thoroughly mix the beef, turnips, barley, and cinnamon in a bowl. Serve.

Variations

> 10½ cups ground or cubed beef (5 pounds)
> ½ cup olive oil
> 5¾ cups cubed turnips
> 5¾ cups cooked barley
> 3½ teaspoons cinnamon (optional)

Protein: Any meat can be substituted for the beef in this recipe, even pork.

Carbohydrates: White or brown rice may be substituted for the barley.

Low-Fat Heart Food

Yield: 3 cups, or 1 serving
Preparation time: 30 minutes
Cooking time: 35 minutes

Holistic veterinarians generally recommend a low-fat diet for a wide range of heart conditions because the hearts of overweight dogs are so taxed. This recipe is lower in fat than the average recipe because turkey breast is a very lean cut of meat and, when boiled, its fat content is reduced further.

I usually explain to clients that there are many heart ailments; what is usually meant by heart disease is high blood pressure or aging of the heart valves. (Unlike human beings, dogs do not suffer from hardening of the arteries.) The heart is the organ responsible for pumping blood through the body, bringing nutrients and oxygen to the tissues and other organs. To prevent heart disease, you want to ensure your dog does not become overweight because extra fat around the heart impedes the heart from working at its fullest capacity.

Also feed your dog tomatoes for their amazing antioxidant property. That helps prevent damage to the heart. In addition, flaxseed oil is an absolute necessity. Flaxseed oil actually thins the blood. It is like liquid drain cleaner!

This particular recipe was created for one of my customers, whose aging pet had an enlarged heart. Although her sweet dog finally passed away, he enjoyed this meal greatly and I think it helped keep him going for longer than he would have otherwise.

1½ cups ground turkey breast (12 ounces)
¾ cup cooked rice, brown or white

¾ cup cooked chopped zucchini
(about 3 medium zucchini)
1 tablespoon dill, dried or fresh

Boil the turkey in water for 30 minutes or until cooked
through. Drain and reserve broth for another use.
Mix the turkey, rice, zucchini, and dill in a bowl and serve.

Variations

Full-Week Recipe

10½ cups ground turkey breast (5 pounds)
5¾ cups cooked rice
5¾ cups cooked chopped zucchini
(10 to 12 medium zucchini)
7 tablespoons dill, dried or fresh

Vegetables: For zucchini, you may substitute yellow squash in
the same proportion.

Davie's Juicy Jiggly-Wiggly Anemia Diet

Yield: 3 cups, or 1 serving
Preparation time: 10 minutes
Cooking time: 25 minutes

When Oscar was rescued as a pup, and shortly after his bout with parvovirus at six weeks old, he was severely anemic. Anemia means there is too little iron in the blood and indicates that not enough iron-carrying red blood cells are present. Though anemia is sometimes a product of surgery, in Oscar's case it resulted from an infestation of fleas and ticks. He had wall-to-wall parasites on his body and they were sucking him dry. It was so bad, when you lifted up his lip his gums looked white.

While the veterinarians in the clinic bathed him, dipped him in medicine, and plucked the ticks off his body for two weeks, he was also recovering from his recent treatment with antibiotics. To compensate nutritionally I fed Oscar broccoli, spinach, liver, and eggs. All of these foods are loaded with iron. The result? Today he is an enormous, healthy monster. When I go to the vet and fill in the clipboard checklist that asks for information like "dog, cat, or other," I always check "other" and write in "half-dog half-dragon."

The aroma of Davie's Juicy Jiggly-Wiggly Anemia Diet will make any dog drool. You'll need skewers and to cook over a gas flame or grill.

1½ cups chopped chicken livers or beef liver (12 ounces)

Pinch of sea salt
1½ cups cooked white rice
½ cup steamed spinach

Thread the chicken or beef livers on skewers. Sear over a
gas-stove flame or a grill, rotating the skewers every 15 seconds. You only want to sear the outside of the liver, not
cook them through, and this happens quickly in a minute
or two. When brown on the outside, immediately take the
livers off the skewers and place them in a dog food bowl.
Add a pinch of sea salt. The meat will begin dripping juices.
Add the rice and spinach and blend well, making sure the
liver juice is spread thoroughly.
Serve at room temperature.

Note: Raisins are another extremely good source of iron. You can always sprinkle five to ten
raisins on top of the food in your dog's bowl.

Variations

Full-Week Recipe

10½ cups chopped chicken livers or beef liver
(5 pounds)
10½ cups cooked white rice
3½ cups steamed spinach
1 tablespoon sea salt

Weight-Loss Recipe

Yield: 3 cups, or 1 serving
Preparation time: 15 minutes
Cooking time: 35 minutes

When Hannah reached five, her metabolism slowed down and she started getting roly-poly. In fact, she looked like a jelly roll, with no neck and short little legs; the extra weight just exacerbated her natural curves. Even though I feed Hannah the same meals as my other two dogs, she cannot handle grains as well as they do, so I serve this, and her weight has gotten back under control.

Caution: Do not feed this recipe and its variations to your dog for more than three weeks without checking with your veterinarian. Long-term weight loss must be supervised.

1½ cups cubed boneless lamb (12 ounces)
2 tablespoons olive oil
¾ cup cooked chopped zucchini (about
    3 medium zucchini)
¾ cup grated carrots (about 3 medium carrots)

Brown the lamb in the olive oil in a large skillet over low heat
    for 30 minutes.
Combine meat, zucchini, and carrots in a mixing bowl. Serve.

Variations

Full-Week Recipe

10½ cups cubed boneless lamb (5 pounds)
½ cup olive oil

5¾ cups cooked chopped zucchini
    (10 to 12 medium zucchini)
5¾ cups grated carrots (10 to 12 medium carrots)

Protein: Use any lean meat except pork, in the same proportion.

Vegetables: You can substitute yellow squash, broccoli, asparagus, Brussels sprouts, and celery for the zucchini in the same proportion. (Note: When cooking celery, boil it for 45 minutes until it is very mushy. My dogs go wild for this aroma.)

Nonmeat Protein Healing Diet

Yield: 3 cups, or 1 serving
Preparation time: 10 minutes
Cooking time: 35 minutes

If you are following the Rotation Diet, this is a main dish that you may serve your dog once a week to give her body a rest from meat protein, which can tax the kidneys and liver. Eggs have the perfect protein of any animal product. You can substitute any other egg meal for this meal in the Rotation Diet.

Because I recommend that you only feed this once a week, I do not give a weekly version here. However, you can hard-boil many eggs and keep them on hand in the refrigerator to make this fresh each day if you choose to serve it more than once in a given week. It takes very little time to prepare.

For the nonmeat Protein Healing Diet, cook the rice in beef, chicken, liver, or vegetable broth. However, as I have discussed elsewhere, broth may make the food too rich for your dog's digestive system. If your dog tolerates the broth, make this recipe as soupy as you want—your dog will enjoy it both ways.

6 large eggs, hard-boiled with shells removed
1½ cups cooked white rice
1 heaping tablespoon cottage cheese
    (any level of fat content)
½ cup broth or more (optional)

Mash the eggs in a bowl. Add the rice and cottage cheese and
blend well. Cool to room temperature and serve.

Variations

Carbohydrates: You may substitute 1½ cups cooked oatmeal or
bulgur wheat for the rice.

Barker's Grub

Colitis Diet

Yield: 3 cups, or 1 serving
Preparation time: 40 minutes
Cooking time: 40 minutes

Colitis is a chronic bowel problem whose treatment requires a bland diet low in vegetables. (Vegetables can irritate the bowel because they contain fiber.) The primary symptom of colitis is bloody diarrhea, usually a result of ulcers in the intestines. Bacteria or parasites can also cause this condition. My dog George once ate the neighbor's garbage and had symptoms of colitis for three weeks. The vomiting and diarrhea are signs that the body is purging itself of a disagreeable substance, such as a toxin, allergen, or infectious agent.

Note: It is critically important to know that your dog may become dehydrated if it is suffering from colitis. A dog that vomits and has diarrhea for forty-eight hours could die. Take your pet to the vet within six or seven hours if symptoms persist.

A good friend of mine has a dog named Sandy who suffers from both colitis and allergies. She was having difficulty striking a balance in the treatment of both conditions. The Rotation Diet exacerbated the colitis, so this recipe helped stabilize Sandy.

Caution: Flaxseed oil or other oil may aggravate colitis. Therefore do not supplement this recipe as usual.

1½ cups cubed or ground lamb (12 ounces)
¾ cup cooked barley
¾ cup boiled and mashed sweet or white potatoes
    (1 to 2½ potatoes)
1 tablespoon dried catnip (optional)

Boil the lamb in 2½ cups water for 30 minutes, until tender. Drain and reserve broth for another use.

Combine the lamb, barley, and potato in a bowl. Stir in the catnip and serve.

NOTE: Catnip promotes digestion. For severe cases of colitis, however, this may not be advisable. Check with your veterinarian.

Variations

Full-Week Recipe

10½ cups ground or cubed lamb (5 pounds)

5¾ cups cooked barley

5¾ cups boiled and mashed sweet or white potatoes (4 to 5½ potatoes)

¼ cup dried catnip (optional)

TNT Constipation Recipe

Yield: 3 cups, or 1 serving
Preparation time: 20 minutes
Cooking time: 40 minutes

Constipation generally occurs when a dog is not getting enough fiber. It is very unlikely that a healthy dog will get constipation if you feed it the Rotation Diet and make sure your dog exercises regularly. If these practices don't work, however, try this TNT Constipation Recipe. It should provide explosive relief.

The secret weapons here are oatmeal and beets. You can add a little extra olive oil until your pet recovers. (Be prepared!)

1½ cups chopped chicken livers (12 ounces)
2 tablespoons olive oil
½ cup chopped beet, unpeeled
1½ cups cooked oatmeal

Brown the chicken livers in the olive oil in a large skillet over
   low heat for approximately 10 minutes.
Boil the beet for approximately 25 to 30 minutes, until soft.
Combine the livers, oatmeal, and beets in a bowl and serve at
   room temperature.

Anti-Cancer Food

Yield: 3 cups, or 1 serving
Preparation time: 10 minutes
Cooking time: 40 minutes

Of all the healing recipes I make, this is the one I make most often. There are so many forms of cancer, and the numbers of dogs that suffer from cancer is staggering. A low-carbohydrate, high-protein, high-fat diet is very important in anti-cancer meals, particularly for dogs undergoing chemotherapy. You also want to use those vegetables that are highest in the antioxidant vitamins and in minerals such as iron.

When a dog has cancer it needs more calories in its diet. Cancer burns energy quickly, and it is important that the dog not lose lean muscle mass, which is ultimately weakening. Your dog will need frequent feedings of high-protein and high-fat food. Your vet may advise you to be wary of grains; avoid noodles and rice in favor of potatoes and sweet potatoes, squash, and pumpkin, because these carbohydrates have more vitamins and minerals, plus they are richer in soluble fiber. Sweet potatoes are one of the more complete foods, rich in nutrients. Also, the more dark leafy green vegetables the dog eats, the better, because of their mineral content, especially iron.

2 cups ground chicken (16 ounces)
4 tablespoons olive oil, divided use
½ cup chopped tomatoes
½ cup water
½ cup cooked chopped broccoli
2 tablespoons cottage cheese
1 tablespoon of flaxseed oil (see Note)

Brown the chicken in 2 tablespoons olive oil in a large skillet over low heat for approximately 30 to 40 minutes.

Sauté the tomatoes in the remaining 2 tablespoons olive oil. Add the water and simmer for 25 minutes.

Combine all the ingredients in a large bowl, cool to room temperature, and serve.

Variations

Full-Week Recipe

14 cups ground chicken (7 pounds)
½ cup olive oil
3½ cups chopped tomatoes
3½ cups cooked chopped broccoli
½ cup cottage cheese
7 tablespoons flaxseed oil (see Note)

NOTE: Because flaxseed oil does not keep well, add it in 1 tablespoon quantities to single-serving portions just prior to serving.

Protein: You may substitute any meat for the chicken except pork. Use beef, lamb, turkey, or liver in the same proportion.

Carbohydrates: If your dog has lost a lot of weight owing to chemotherapy, add in complex carbohydrates such as 1½ cups cooked sweet potato, pumpkin, spaghetti squash, or acorn squash. Otherwise, I don't recommend using any carbohydrates in this recipe.

Kidney Healing Meal

Yield: 3 cups, or 1 serving
Preparation time: 20 minutes
Cooking time: 20 minutes

This is my second-most-frequently requested healing recipe for dogs—for those who are too often afflicted with kidney disease. This recipe is proportionally low in protein. Make it as soupy with broth as you can; the dog's kidneys need to be flushed out.

1 cup ground beef (8 ounces)
2 tablespoons olive oil
2 cups cooked white rice
½ cup (or more) beef broth (see page 121)

Brown the beef in the olive oil in a large skillet over low heat
  until cooked through, approximately 20 minutes.
Combine the beef and rice in a mixing bowl with the beef broth.
Cool to room temperature and serve.

Variations

Full-Week Recipe

7 cups ground beef (3½ pounds)
½ cup olive oil
14 cups cooked white rice
3½ cups beef broth

Protein: You may substitute ground chicken or turkey for the beef in the same proportions. Make the broth consistent with the meat—that is, use chicken broth for a chicken dish and turkey broth with turkey.

Diabetes Meal

Yield: 3 cups, or 1 serving
Preparation time: 15 minutes
Cooking time: 45 minutes

Diabetes is a serious condition yet one that can easily be controlled with correct supervision. Before you use this recipe or make any decisions about what to feed your dog, consult your veterinarian. There are many forms of diabetes, and diabetic dogs should be under the regular attention of a veterinarian to monitor blood insulin levels. The merits of this Diabetes Meal are that it is low in fat, low in carbohydrates, and high in protein.

¼ cup red lentils
1½ cups cubed turkey (12 ounces)
1¾ cups sliced green beans (preferably fresh,
   but frozen may be substituted)

Boil the lentils in water to cover for 30 minutes or until mushy.

Boil the turkey in water to cover until cooked through, approximately 10 to 15 minutes. Drain and reserve broth for another use. Place meat in a large bowl.

Boil the green beans for 10 minutes or until soft. (If you're using frozen green beans, follow the packaging instructions.)

Add the lentils and beans to the meat, combine well, and serve at room temperature.

Variations

Full-Week Recipe

        1¾ cups red lentils
        10½ cups ground or cubed turkey (5 pounds)
        12¼ cups green beans

Aggression Reduction Meal

Yield: 3 cups, or 1 serving
Preparation time: 30 minutes
Cooking time: 15 minutes

High-fat foods have been proven to reduce aggression. In this recipe, I have chosen fatty pork; however, you can substitute any fatty meat. Because I have noticed that my dogs' stomachs do not tolerate pork well, I rarely use it; the only cuts I use are bacon—for flavor—and pork chops.

Experiment with this recipe and see how well your own dog digests pork. If it is not suitable, use lamb or beef.

1½ cups cubed extra-fatty pork (12 ounces)
2 tablespoons olive oil
1½ cups cooked elbow macaroni
½ cup mashed potatoes (1 or 2 potatoes)
1½ tablespoons dill, fresh or dried
1½ tablespoons flaxseed oil (see Note)
1½ tablespoons Chinese parsley (cilantro),
 fresh or dried

Brown the pork in the olive oil in a large skillet over low heat
 for 30 to 40 minutes or until cooked through.
Combine the pork, macaroni, mashed potatoes, dill, and
 cilantro in a large mixing bowl. Cool to room temperature,
 and add the flaxseed oil just prior to serving.

Variations

Full-Week Recipe

10½ cups extra-fatty pork (5 pounds)

½ cup olive oil

10½ cups cooked elbow macaroni

3½ cups mashed potatoes (2½ to 3 potatoes)

¼ cup flaxseed oil (see Note)

¼ cup plus 3 tablespoons dill, fresh or dried

10 tablespoons Chinese parsley, fresh or dried

NOTE: The flaxseed oil is added here as a main ingredient and not a supplement. In this case, the dog needs the extra fatty acids flaxseed provides.

Protein: You may substitute any fatty meat for the pork. Try 1½ cups fatty lamb or beef.

Carbohydrates: Of course, you can substitute any pasta for the elbow macaroni. You may also substitute 1½ cups cooked rice, either white or brown.

Arthritis Be Gone

Yield: 3 cups, or 1 serving
Preparation time: 20 minutes
Cooking time: 40 minutes

A while back my horse was diagnosed with arthritis. She had been a racehorse for many years before becoming mine, and her condition resulted from the constant impact of running on a track. My veterinarian told me to give her yucca root as a dietary supplement to reduce the inflammation. Because I had spent so many years riding and falling off horses, I suffer from arthritis, too. Yucca also helped me enormously. I think it tastes better than potatoes.

Later, I incorporated this anti-inflammatory root into my recipe for dogs, figuring that if it worked for humans and horses, why not dogs? The results of my experiment have been proven by positive experience. Not only do my customers report that their dogs thrive on Arthritis Be Gone, but Hannah does well on it. Nutritionally, yucca is a good source of complex carbohydrates.

Caution: Yucca root, which you can find in almost any major supermarket today, comes with inedible wax on the outside. You must remove the peel before cooking.

1½ cups ground turkey (12 ounces)
2 tablespoons olive oil
1½ cups peeled and cubed yucca root
½ cup yellow squash
1 tablespoon cartilage (optional supplement)

Brown the ground turkey in the olive oil in a large skillet over
    low heat for approximately 30 minutes.
Boil the yucca in water for 30 minutes, until tender.
Boil the yellow squash in water for 20 minutes, until tender.
Combine the turkey, yucca, and squash in a mixing bowl.
    Cool to room temperature. If using, sprinkle 1 tablespoon
    of cartilage over the mix before serving.

Variations

Full-Week Recipe: If you are supplementing this dish with cartilage,
do so just prior to serving.

> 10½ cups ground turkey (5 pounds)
> ½ cup olive oil
> 10½ cups peeled and cubed yucca root
> 3½ cups cubed yellow squash
> 7 tablespoons cartilage (optional supplement)

Protein: You may substitute any other meat for the ground
turkey.

Note: You can find cartilage at the health food store, either chicken, shark, or another kind.

Rudy's Beet Stew

Yield: 3 cups, or 1 serving
Preparation time: 10 minutes
Cooking time: 45 minutes

This is a variation on my mom's home cooking. Besides being really yummy, it is a purifier that flushes out the digestive system. Beets are high in fiber, and although dogs don't tolerate fiber all that well, when the beets are cooked in this fashion the dogs' systems seem to handle it okay. Beets are also high in antioxidant vitamin C.

4 cups water
1½ cups cubed or ground extra-fatty lamb (12 ounces)
1 cup cubed beets
½ cup barley
1 garlic clove, finely chopped
1 teaspoon oregano, fresh or dried
½ cup dry bread crumbs

Bring the water to a boil in a large pot. Add the lamb, beets, barley, garlic, and oregano. Continue boiling until all the ingredients are well cooked through and through, approximately 45 minutes. This is a stew, so it should be soupy.

Just before serving, top with bread crumbs.

Variations

Full-Week Recipe: And add the bread crumbs after you take the single portion out of the freezer.

> 7 quarts water
> 10½ cups cubed or ground lamb (5 pounds)
> 7 cups cubed beets
> 3½ cups barley
> 7 garlic cloves
> ¼ cup oregano, fresh or dried
> 3½ cups dry bread crumbs

Protein: For the lamb you may substitute ground beef or turkey in the same proportion.

Vegetables: You may also cook and add the beet greens to the stew, if you so choose, as an extra source of nutrients. However, do not measure these in place of the beet root!

Detox Italian Style

Yield: 3 cups, or 1 serving
Preparation time: 10 minutes
Cooking time: 40 minutes

Tomatoes! Nothing compares to their antioxidant properties. Every time you turn around these days, another article is exploring the miraculous phytochemicals in these fruits that masquerade as vegetables. Interestingly, it is also true that the antioxidants they contain, such as vitamin C, are intensified—not lessened—when they are cooked. This recipe uses fresh tomatoes and ground beef Italian style, over pasta. Buon appetito!

1½ cups extra-fatty ground beef (12 ounces)
3 tablespoons olive oil
¾ cup spaghetti noodles or angel hair pasta
¾ cup finely chopped fresh tomatoes
¼ cup water
1 garlic clove, minced
½ teaspoon oregano, fresh or dried
1 tablespoon fresh parsley, finely chopped

Brown the beef in 1 tablespoon olive oil in a large skillet over low heat for approximately 30 minutes, until cooked through. Stir often.

Boil the spaghetti or angel hair pasta until tender, following the instructions on the package. (Spaghetti takes approximately 12 minutes to cook, whereas angel hair pasta, which is finer, takes approximately 6 minutes.)

Sauté the chopped tomatoes in the remaining 2 tablespoons
of olive oil in a large skillet over low heat until soft, approximately 20 minutes. Add the water and cook for another
5 minutes.

Toss all the ingredients together in a mixing bowl and serve.

Variations

Full-Week Recipe

10½ cups ground beef (5 pounds)
¾ cup olive oil
5¾ cups noodles
5¾ cups finely chopped fresh tomatoes
1¾ cups water
7 garlic cloves
3½ teaspoons oregano, fresh or dried
¼ cup fresh parsley, finely chopped

Protein: The only meat I would substitute for ground beef
would be ground turkey.

Carbohydrates: Use whatever noodles are the easiest for you, or
which you have handy.

TREATS

Basic Vegetarian Cookie Recipe

Charly's Apple—Peanut Butter Treats

Carrot—Peanut Butter Treats

Hannah Banana Treats

Tasty Anti-Allergy Cookies

The five cookie recipes in this section are light and easy to prepare. They also keep well over time. Try them all; they're sure to satisfy any canine that likes snacking. I've even added one for dogs with wheat allergies.

Among other benefits, dog training can become a whole lot easier with treats. Dogs will be much more willing to cooperate if they know they are well cared for and feel rewarded. For training exercises, like sitting, staying, and fetching, treats help make an impression. To the dog, the reward comes from having something special. Truthfully, verbal and nonverbal praise can be just as effective as snacks.

You do not want a dog to become obese from oversnacking. But perhaps the treats can become positive sources of nourishment in the proper moment. While dog cookies should never substitute for regular meals, think of homemade treats as one way to give your dog the vegetables he needs. You can also train your dog using treats such as carrot sticks or green beans.

Basic Vegetarian Cookie Recipe

Yield: 5¾ pounds, or 1-month supply
Preparation time: 15 minutes
Cooking time: 1½ hours

Growing up and working as a stable hand, I first got interested in treats for horses, who loved apples and oats with molasses. Later, when I began developing meals for dogs, I wanted to get away from meat-based biscuits or cookies and use a complement to the protein that they were already getting in good doses from their main dishes. My dogs went nuts for the horse treats.

The Basic Vegetarian Cookie Recipe is the result of my "dog-idizing" of the horse recipe. Even though it is never a substitute for vegetables at regular mealtimes, it is a terrific added source of vegetable nutrients that makes your pets feel special and well loved.

These cookies have a long shelf life, and one batch can stretch throughout an entire month so long as they are given room to breathe in a clean environment. You may keep them in a paper bag. Another good way to make a breathing cookie jar is to transform an old teakettle or teapot. (Make sure it is rust free.) These make wonderful baked gifts.

6 cups whole-wheat flour
10 cups oatmeal, traditional or instant
1 tablespoon baking powder
8 cups mashed cooked sweet potatoes
    (7 to 8 potatoes)
5 tablespoons blackstrap molasses

5 heaping tablespoons peanut butter (any kind)
4 tablespoons olive oil
2 cups lukewarm water

Preheat the oven to 350 degrees. Combine the flour, oats, and baking powder in an 8-quart capacity mixing bowl. Add the sweet potatoes, molasses, peanut butter, and olive oil, stirring with a wooden spoon and/or kneading with your hands as necessary. Finally, add the lukewarm water 1 cup at a time. Continue to mix well until the batter is smooth and there are no dry clumps remaining.

Lightly dust a flat surface with flour so the dough won't stick. Roll the cookie dough flat, spreading it evenly to a ½-inch thickness. Cut the dough with any type and size of cookie cutter. Put the dough shapes on nonstick or greased cookie sheets and bake for 30 to 40 minutes. Cookies will be done when they are golden brown on the edges. Remove from oven. Let cool and serve.

NOTE: Since every oven is different, check the cookies every 10 to 15 minutes to make sure that they are not overbaking.

Charly's Apple—Peanut Butter Treats

Yield: 5¾ pounds of treats, or 1-month supply
Preparation time: 10 minutes
Cooking time: 1½ hours

Peanut butter is an ideal snack food because it is rich in fatty acids and protein, and dogs love that salty flavor. Less "cruel" than putting a sticky dab on their noses—and watching them lick it off—is incorporating it into a treat recipe with the sweet complement of apples or the variation of carrots. I have named this recipe in honor of my pet Charly who, while alive, absolutely adored peanut butter.

This is also aromatherapy. Once the two main ingredients are baked together, your house will be saturated with a delicious scent.

6 cups whole-wheat flour
10 cups oatmeal, traditional or instant
1 tablespoon baking powder
4 cups apples, finely grated in a food processor
   (5 to 6 medium apples)
5 tablespoons blackstrap molasses
10 heaping tablespoons peanut butter (any kind)
4 tablespoons olive oil
2 cups lukewarm water

Preheat the oven to 350 degrees. Combine the flour, oats, and baking powder in an 8-quart mixing bowl. Then add the grated apples, molasses, peanut butter, and olive oil, stirring with a wooden spoon and/or kneading with your hands as necessary. Add the lukewarm water 1 cup at a time. Continue to mix well until the batter is smooth and there are no dry clumps remaining.

Lightly dust a flat surface with flour so the dough won't stick. Roll the cookie dough flat, spreading it evenly to a ½-inch thickness. Cut the dough with any type and size of cookie cutter. Put the dough shapes on nonstick or greased cookie sheets and bake for 30 to 40 minutes. Cookies will be done when they are golden brown on the edges. Remove from oven. Let cool and serve.

Variation: Carrot—Peanut Butter Treats

Substitute 4 cups grated carrots for the apples. The cooking instructions are the same.

Hannah Banana Treats

Yield: 5¾ pounds of treats, or 1-month supply
Preparation time: 10 minutes
Cooking time: 1½ hours

I had always struggled to persuade Hannah to eat bananas because George loved them—and it is so much easier if all your dogs eat the same thing! But she turned up her wet nose at them. To this day, the only way she likes bananas is in these cookies. Bananas are a fantastic source of potassium (and raw, they are good for an upset stomach).

6 cups whole-wheat flour
6 cups rice flour
10 cups oatmeal, traditional or instant

1 tablespoon baking powder
8 cups mashed bananas (10 to 12 bananas)
5 tablespoons blackstrap molasses
5 heaping tablespoons peanut butter (any kind)
4 tablespoons olive oil
2 cups lukewarm water

Preheat the oven to 350 degrees. Combine the flours, oats, and baking powder in an 8-quart mixing bowl. Add the mashed bananas, molasses, peanut butter, and olive oil, stirring with a wooden spoon and/or kneading with your hands as necessary. Add the lukewarm water 1 cup at a time. Continue to mix well, until the batter is smooth and there are no dry clumps remaining.

Lightly dust a flat surface with flour so the dough won't stick. Roll the cookie dough flat, spreading it evenly to a ½-inch thickness. Cut the dough with any type and size of cookie cutter. Put the dough shapes on nonstick or greased cookie sheets and bake for 30 to 40 minutes. Cookies will be done when they are golden brown on the edges. Remove from oven. Let cool and serve.

Tasty Anti-Allergy Cookies

Yield: 4 to 5 pounds, or 1-month supply
Preparation time: 10 minutes
Cooking time: 1½ hours

I get many calls from clients and vets requesting wheat-free recipes for dogs with allergies. While I created this treat recipe especially for these animals, all dogs love it.

6 cups cubed yellow squash
   (10 to 12 medium squash)
2 cups frozen green peas
5 tablespoons blackstrap molasses
4 tablespoons olive oil
12 cups rice flour
1 tablespoon baking powder
2 cups lukewarm water

Preheat the oven to 350 degrees. Boil the yellow squash for approximately 20 minutes, until mushy. Drain and mash in a large bowl; then mix in the peas, molasses, and olive oil.

Gradually add in the rice flour 1 cup at a time, and the baking powder, alternating with half-cups of the water and stirring well until smooth. When it becomes drier and more doughy, knead the mixture with your hands, making sure that no clumps remain.

Lightly dust a flat surface with flour so the dough won't stick. Roll the cookie dough flat, spreading it evenly to a ½-inch thickness. Cut the dough with any type and size of cookie cutter. Put the dough shapes on nonstick or greased cookie sheets and bake for 30 to 35 minutes. Cookies will be done when they are golden on the edges. Remove from oven. Let cool and serve.

Resources

The organizations, publications, and Web sites listed below are resources intended to assist you in caring for your dog. I would love to hear from you, so I begin with my own:

> *Barker's Grub*
> PO Box 190
> Cabin John, MD 20818
> Phone/fax: (301) 229-2620

VETERINARY MEDICINE

> *Academy of Veterinary Homeopathy*
> 751 NE 168th Street
> North Miami Beach, FL 33162-2427
> (305) 653-7244
> Fax: (305) 652-1590
> www.acadvethom.org

An organization founded by Dr. Richard H. Pitcairn to advance veterinary homeopathy in the United States and to train and certify homeopathic veterinarians.

> *International Association of Veterinary Homeopathy*
> 334 Knollwood Lane
> Woodstock, GA 30188
> (770) 516-5954
> Fax: (770) 516-7622

> *American Holistic Veterinary Medical Association*
> 2214 Old Emmorton Road
> Bel Air, MD 21015

(410) 569-0795
Fax: (410) 569-2346
Email: AHVMA@compuserve.com

Contact this organization to find the name of a holistic veterinarian in your area.

American Academy of Veterinary Acupuncture
PO Box 419
Hygiene, CO 80533-0419
http://aava.org

An organization that promotes veterinary acupuncture and traditional Chinese medicine and trains veterinarians in these disciplines.

AMERICAN VETERINARY CHIROPRACTIC ASSOCIATION

Animal Chiropractic Center
623 Main Street
Hillsdale, IL 61257
(309) 658-2920
Fax: (309) 658-2622

Ani-Med Phone Information Service of the
  American Society for the Prevention of Cruelty
  to Animals (ASPCA)
(888) 252-7381 [a toll-free call]

Using a touchtone phone, you can get recorded information about dog care for wide-ranging topics from pet-proofing the house to hot-weather tips, trimming nails, housebreaking, worms, and aggression.

American Animal Hospital Association
(800) 883-6301 [a toll-free call]
www.healthypet.com

Established in 1933, this is an organization of more than 17,000 veterinary care providers, which can help you locate an emergency animal medical center in a crisis.

HERBS AND FLOWER ESSENCES

> *Equilite, Inc.*
> Ardsley, NY
> (800) 942-LYTE [a toll-free call]
> (914) 693-2553

This business custom-makes herbal remedies and flower essences for dogs and cats with behavioral disorders.

> *Nelson Bach USA, Ltd.*
> Wilmington, MA
> (800) 319-9151 [a toll-free call]
> (978) 988-3833

They make the famous Bach flower essences of which Rescue Remedy is especially handy.

> *Flower Essences Services*
> Nevada City, CA
> (800) 548-0075 [a toll-free call]
> (530) 265-0258

Another source of herbs and flower essences.

PERIODICALS

> *The Whole Dog Journal*
> 1175 Regent Street
> Alameda, CA 94501
> (510) 749-1080
> Fax: (510) 749-4905

Ian Dunbar, dog trainer and author of the wonderful book *Dog Behavior*, publishes this monthly magazine.

> *Canine Health Naturally*
> PO Box 69, Dept C
> Lions Bay, BC V0N 2E0
> CANADA
> (604) 921-7784
> www.prodogs.com

> *Natural Rearing Newsletter*
> (541) 899-2080
> Fax: (541) 899-3414
> www.naturalrearing.com

RESCUE GROUPS

> *American Society for the Prevention of Cruelty*
> *to Animals*
> 424 East 92nd Street
> New York, NY 10128–6804
> (212) 876-7700
> www.aspca.org

Founded in 1866, the ASPCA was the first humane organization in the Western Hemisphere. To find your national chapter go to their Web site or check your local yellow pages. The Web site has links to organizations in every state.

> *Humane Society of the United States*
> National Headquarters
> 2100 L Street, NW
> Washington, DC 20007
> (202) 452-1100
> www.hsus.org

Central States: IL, KY, MN, NC, TN, and WI. (630) 357-7015

Great Lakes: IN, MI, OH, and WV. (419) 352-5141

Mid-Atlantic: DE, NJ, NY, and PA. (973) 927-5611

New England: CT, MA, ME, NH, RI, VT. (802) 368-2790

Northern Rockies: ID, MT, ND, SD, and WY. (406) 255-7161

Southeast: AL. FL, GA, MS, and SC. (850) 386-3435

Southwest: AR, AZ, CO, LA, NM, OK, TX, and UT. (972) 488-2964

West Coast: CA, NV, OR, and WA. (916) 344-1710

ANIMAL SHELTERS

How can you find your local shelter? The easiest place to start is your phone book. Animal shelters are called by a variety of names, so look under listings such as "Humane Society," "Animal Shelter," or "Animal Control." Public animal control and care facilities are often listed under the city or county health department or police department.

Save Our Strays
www.saveourstrays.com

A Web site with links to many others, including those in your local area.

Canine Connections—Breed Rescue Information
www.canine-connections.com/rescue

Dog Zone
www.dogzone.com/rescue

Cyber Pet—Rescue
www.cyberpet.com

This is an Internet site with myriad useful articles and links about dogs, as well as links to rescue organizations throughout the United States and Canada.

Metro Pets On-line
www.metropets.org/mmm
(301) 490-5266

This Maryland-based organization helps people find the right dog for them.

National Breed Club Rescue
www.akc.org/breed/rescue.cfm

The American Kennel Club sponsors rescues for pure-breed dogs through this Web site. Check them out if you are dreaming of adopting a specific breed. There are separate links for myriad breeds of dogs.

The Paw Pad
PO Box 70060 SW
Washington, DC 20024
(202) 546-3177
Email: ThePawPad@aol.com

This is a rescue organization I am involved with in Washington, DC.

LOW-COST SPAYING/NEUTERING

Spaying/neutering is a one-time cost associated with responsible pet ownership. Animal advocates generally consider these relatively simple surgical procedures essential pet birth control. If you cannot immediately afford the surgery, your veterinarian might be willing to work out a payment plan with you. Likewise, your local shelter may operate a spay/neuter clinic or know of a local clinic that offers subsidized services. Sometimes shelters offer vouchers for discount spaying/neutering by cooperating local veterinarians.

> *Spay USA*
> (800) 248-SPAY (7729) [a toll-free call]

> A national spay/neuter referral network that may be
> able to direct you to subsidized spay/neuter clinics
> in your area.

SERVICE DOGS
Service dogs can benefit people with disabilities such as spinal cord or head trauma, visual or hearing deficits, arthritis, ataxia/poor balance, multiple sclerosis, cerebral palsy, muscular dystrophy, spina bifida, seizure disorders, sickle cell anemia, cardiopulmonary disease, arteriovascular disease (secondary to diabetes), recovery from trauma or depression, AIDS, chronic pain, anxiety, and neuroses. They can be trained to perform numerous tasks, some of which are leading, sound discrimination, general assistance, sense and alert, and emotional support.

> *Delta Society*
> (800) 869-6898 [a toll-free call]
> www.petsforum.com/deltasociety/default.html

This organization is dedicated to the pet-human bond and has much valuable information and links to service dog providers.

> *The Seeing Eye, Inc.*
> (973) 539-4425
> www.seeingeye.org

Established in 1929, this is one of the oldest training schools for guide dogs.

> *Pilot Dogs, Inc.*
> 625 West Town Street

Columbus, OH 43215
(614) 221-63637
Fax: (614) 221-1577
http://pilotdogs.org

Members of this organization breed and train dogs for blind owners.

Canine Companions for Independence
National Headquarters
PO Box 446
Santa Rosa, CA 95402-0446
(800) 572-2275 [a toll-free call for TDD/Voice]
www.caninecompanions.org

A nonprofit organization that provides highly trained assistance dogs to people with disabilities and to professional caregivers. They have regional offices throughout the United States and are always seeking loving homes for puppy fostering.

Paws With A Cause
4646 South Division
Wayland, MI 49348
(616) 877-PAWS (7297) [TDD/Voice]
(800) 253-PAWS (7297) [a toll-free call for
TDD/Voice]
Fax: (616) 877-0248
www.pawswithacause.org

Paws With A Cause trains assistance dogs nationally for people with disabilities and provides lifetime team support which encourages independence. Paws promotes awareness through education.

Recommended Reading

Bauer, Nora Kilgore. *Adopting a Great Dog*. Neptune City, NJ: T. F. H. Publications, 1997.

Belfield, Wendell O., and Martin Zucker. Foreword by Linus Pauling. *How to Have a Healthier Dog*. San Jose, CA: Orthomolecular Specialties, 1981.

Cusick, William D. *Canine Nutrition*. Wilsonville, OR: Doral Publishing, 1997.

Derrico, Karen. *Unforgettable Mutts*. Troutdale, OR: NewSage Press, 1999.

Dunbar, Ian. *Dog Behavior*. Foster City, CA: IDG Books, 1998.

Fox, Michael W. *The Healing Touch*. New York: Newmarket Press, 1990.

——. *Understanding Your Dog*. New York: St. Martin's Press, 1992.

——. *Superdog*. Foster City, CA: IDG Books Worldwide, 1996.

Lewis, Lon D., Mark Morris, Jr., and Michael S. Hand. *Small Animal Clinical Nutrition, III*. Topeka, KS: Mark Morris Associates, 1987.

Mindell, Earl, and Elizabeth Renaghan. *Earl Mindell's Nutrition and Health for Dogs*. Rocklin, CA: Prima Publishing, 1998.

Palika, Liz. *The Consumer's Guide to Dog Food*. New York: Howell Book House, 1996.

Pitcairn, Richard H., and Susan Hubble Pitcairn. *Dr. Pitcairn's Complete Guide to Natural Health for Cats and Dogs*. Emmaus, PA: Rodale Press, 1995.

Schoen, Alan, and Pam Proctor. *Love, Miracles, and Animal Healing*. New York: Fireside, 1996.

Volhard, Wendy, and Kerry Brown. *The Holistic Guide for a Healthy Dog*. New York: Howell Book House, 1995.

Index

dog food. *See* natural diet;
processed dog food
dogs
hypersensitive, 84, 110
Natural (mixed breed), 28,
37–40
older, 81
pregnant and lactating, 73,
79–80, 112
puppies, 73, 80–81, 123
purebred, 39–48
from shelter, 81–82
*Dr. Pitcairn's Complete Guide
to Natural Health for Dogs
and Cats* (Pitcairn and
Pitcairn), 152
dry food, 30–31

E

*Earl Mindell's Nutrition and
Health for Dogs* (Mindell
and Reneghan), 152
Easter Recipe, 143–44
Egg(s)
in Blue Moon Salmon Special,
137–38
in Daily Calcium Supplement,
76
in Easter Recipe, 143–44
Eggshell Powder, 75
in Nonmeat Protein Healing
Diet, 165–66
and Turkey Puppy Food, 126
Eggshell Powder, 75
English Springer Spaniel, 43
enzyme supplements, 76–77
epilepsy, 38, 52

F

Falconer, William, 28
fasting, 111
fat, dietary, 52, 56–57, 89, 175
feces eating, 90–91
feeding
adopted shelter dogs, 81–82
forbidden foods, 103–4
frequency, 101–3
healing dogs, 84
older dogs, 81
portions, 101–3, 119
pregnant and lactating females,
79–80
puppies, 80
fiber, 55–56, 179
Field Spaniel, 43
flaxseed oil
buying, 57, 100
effect on colitis, 167
effect on kidney damage, 87
health benefits from, 159
in weekly diet, 69, 70, 71
fleas, 28, 85, 161
Florazyme, 77, 91
Fox, Michael W., 22, 29, 35,
77, 153
fruit
in natural diet, 54–55, 56
preparing, for recipes, 116–17
types of, in recipes, 99
washing, 98

G

garbage eating, 91–92
gastrointestinal problems, 85–86,
105

M

macronutrients, 52–57
magnesium, 52, 63–64
main dish recipes, 128–49
Malamute, Alaskan, 45
Maniet, Monique, 21, 36, 152–53
Marder, Amy, 104
marrow bones, 96, 97
meat. *See* Beef; Lamb
micronutrients, 57–65
minerals, 62–65
mixed breeds. *See* natural dogs
Monthly Rotation Diet, 112
Moon Dog Mix: Beef and Potato,
    129–30

N

natural diet. *See also* recipes
    carbohydrates in, 54–55
    emotional benefits from,
      35–37
    fats in, 56–57
    fiber in, 55–56
    immune-boosting effect of, 28,
      36
    minerals in, 62–65
    planning, worksheet for, 49
    as preventative nutrition, 24
    protein in, 53–54
    transitioning to, 104–8
    vitamins in, 57–61
    water in, 66–67
    whole-foods in, 67–68
Natural Dogs
    ancestral diet, 28, 37–38
    dietary needs, 39–40
    genetic attributes, 39–40

neutering and spaying clinics,
    196–97
Nonmeat Protein Healing Diet,
    165–66
nutrients. *See* minerals; vitamins
nutrition, preventative, 24, 36,
    151–53
nutrition, restorative, 153–54
nutrition worksheet, 49
nutritional yeast, 72, 74, 77, 85

O

Old English Sheepdog, 46
older dogs, 81
omega-3 fatty acids, 56–57, 71
onions, 104

P

Peanut Butter
    –Apple Treats, Charly's, 186–87
    in Basic Vegetarian Cookie
      Recipe, 184–85
    –Carrot Treats, 187
    in Hannah Banana Treats, 187–88
pesticides, 68
pet food industry, 26–27, 29
pet therapy, 36
pica, 90–91
pigs' ears, 31, 103
Pit Bull Terrier, 44
poisoning, 87–88
Poodle, Standard, 44
pregnant females, 73, 79–80, 112
preservatives, in dog food, 25–26, 31
preventative nutrition, 24, 36,
    151–53